P9-DNS-010

MAN IN MODERN FICTION

*Some Minority Opinions
on Contemporary
American Writing*

Man in Modern Fiction

Tinkers and Genius:
The Story of the Yankee Inventors

Vermont: A History of the Green Mountain State

George Bernard Shaw: Critic of Western Morale

Brothers Divided (novel)

A Star Pointed North (novel)

John Milton

A Pageant of the Theatre

MAN
IN MODERN
FICTION

Some Minority Opinions
on Contemporary
American Writing

BY EDMUND FULLER

RANDOM HOUSE • NEW YORK

813

Acknowledgments

The author wishes to thank the following writers and publishers for permission to quote from their books as listed below:

John W. Aldridge for *After the Lost Generation* and *In Search of Heresy;* Harper & Brothers for *Ape and Essence,* by Aldous Huxley; The Macmillan Co. for *Mere Christianity,* by C. S. Lewis; Norman Mailer and *Dissent* Magazine for "The White Negro," by Norman Mailer; New Directions for "Desire and the Black Masseur," from *One Arm and Other Stories,* by Tennessee Williams (Copyright, 1947, by Tennessee Williams); Edmund Wilson and *The New Yorker* for Mr. Wilson's review of *A Skeleton Key to Finnegans Wake;* G. P. Putnam's Sons for *The Deer Park,* by Norman Mailer; Philip Wylie and Rinehart & Co. for *Opus 21,* by Philip Wylie; Charles Scribner's Sons for *From Here to Eternity* and *Some Came Running,* by

James Jones, *James Joyce*, by W. Y. Tindall, and *Look Homeward, Angel*, by Thomas Wolfe; Simon & Schuster for *The Organization Man*, by William H. Whyte, Jr.; The Viking Press for *On the Road*, by Jack Kerouac, and *East of Eden*, by John Steinbeck; Herman Wouk for *Aurora Dawn*.

For Ann

Contents

. . . They no longer said of a work of art that it was good or bad, true or false, intelligent or idiotic. They said:

"It may be so. . . . Nothing is impossible. . . . I don't know. . . . I wash my hands of it."

If some objectionable piece were put up, they did not say:

"That is nasty rubbish!"

They said:

"Sir Sganarelle, please do not talk like that. Our philosophy bids us talk of everything open-mindedly: and therefore you ought not to say: 'That is nasty rubbish!' but: 'It seems to me that that is nasty rubbish. . . . But it is not certain that it is so. It may be a masterpiece. Who can say that it is not?' "

—ROMAIN ROLLAND

Preface

This is an age of verbal glut. The printed word rolls
from presses in newspapers, magazines slick and pulp,
comics, and books hard-bound or paper-covered. We
are denuding much of our timberland for the propa-
gation of Bat Man and Mickey Spillane. The spoken
word (which generally gets itself down on paper first)
keeps pace with or exceeds the printed one in the media
of radio, television, and motion pictures.

There were times past when facility of language was
esteemed a great gift and a tolerably rare one, when
it was seldom found unless coupled with some reasonable measure of capacity, talent, or wisdom. Facility with words, mere articulateness, never was in itself
a sound basis upon which to assume merit, but never
has it been less so than today.

This rank proliferation of the printed page includes
contemporary fiction. The output is enormous. The
life span of many of the novels produced is about that
of a fruit fly. Still, on they come. The vagaries of the
publishing business, in which the fiction market fluc-

tuates somewhat, affect the output only to a slight degree.

I spent some years as editor of a publishing house. I remember one of those crank letters that all publishers receive, this one a query concerning a manuscript from an author who wanted to know how much it would cost to have it "published into a book." That comic-pathetic phrase has stayed with me ever since. There are many items on the market, fiction and non-fiction, that are books only because literally they have been "published into books."

So far as writing is concerned, there are a good many men and women around who can write a novel in the sense of producing something sufficiently articulate, and with enough story fabric, to induce a publisher to put it on the market. But there are relatively few who are able to *think* a novel. It is in the area of concept that contemporary fiction is anemic. Only a minority of our novelists have something clear to say, and of these a dismaying number have emphatic things to say of a virulently destructive and anti-social character.

That our age will so readily accept certain superficial glibnesses in literary production is a corollary of the fact that it will accept the same superficialities and glibnesses in the human personality. In the long run, the work is the artist and the artist is the work. It is possible for the artist's work to represent considerably less than his potential, but it is not possible for it to represent more than he is.

This book examines a number of aspects of contemporary fiction. As a critic I am much more interested in what a writer is saying than in the manner in which it is said. Naturally a total separation of thought and expression is not possible. Of course, to say anything extremely well is better than to say it ineptly.

That aspect of modern writing that concerns me most deeply is the vision or image of man, the conception of the nature of man, found in it. I could not have this concern had I not some perspective on man as my frame of reference; for me it is that image of man that is found in the Judeo-Christian tradition, which still primarily influences our moral and ethical thought, and has not become in any way obsolete, though we might be led to think so by dwelling long in the inner worlds of certain of our writers.

I feel that a corrupted and debased image of man has become current and become influential through the persuasiveness and literary skills of some of its projectors. A work of art is always taken to be representative, and unless clear limits are set for the scope of the representation within any work, it is assumed to be more or less universal. There are corrupted and debased men; there have always been and will always be such. It is possible, and now fashionable, in some sets, to portray such men with a tacit assumption or bold implication not that they are particular but that the essential nature of man is revealed in them. It is the often unrecognized, sweeping assumptions of this kind that I challenge.

The view of man for which I am arguing here is no guarantee of literary merit. Neither is its absence related to any lack of artistry. Obviously we can be pious or patriotic—and hideously mediocre as artists. Also it is possible to be immensely gifted creatively and to project a profound distortion of reality. Nevertheless, while man remains the center of his own literary scrutiny, an analysis of the image or doctrine of man inherent in any work must always be a major element in criticism.

In these pages, some parts of which have been published previously, I bring under attack certain writers and books for reasons which sometimes might factitiously appear to coincide with moralistic, repressive, and conventional attacks upon them. As a result, I have now and then found myself more in need of defense against those who thought they agreed with me than against those who disagreed. I have occasionally and mistakenly been applauded as a spokesman for respectability and so-called "decent literature."

Nothing could be further from the mark. I yield to no one on the point of non-respectability. I believe that no close reading of this book can detect repressiveness, prudery, or puritanism as the basis of my harshest criticisms of any book or writer—but a philosophy, a view of man, I will challenge.

I would be a party to nothing that would have suppressed or bowdlerized the sometimes majestic "indecencies" encountered in Aristophanes, Plautus, Rabelais, Shakespeare, Swift, or for that matter, Joyce. I cherish, and indeed am concerned to protect, the vast freedom in language and subject enjoyed by the writer today as the fruit of the fight of several generations. The works of Sacher-Masoch and De Sade are clearly in the clinical category some superficial aspects of which are decried in one of the ensuing chapters—indeed, they contributed to our clinical vocabulary.

In any instance, the things which I am attacking, if I am right about them, cannot be met by censorship but can only be scorned or laughed out of face. At the same time I distinctly attack the canon of critical values which elevates the man-degrading books to claims of literary-artistic eminence. In this connection I have found a few words to say about National Book Award juries thus far in the history of that accolade.

Conventional morality and respectability were rejected by Jesus Himself as the basis of judgment of the hearts of men and women in the struggle of Good with Evil. The creative thinker, which is to say the true artist, always has been at odds with conventional appraisals and has refused to work within or conform to what conventionality has considered acceptable.

My criteria for justification in the artist's free choice of his materials are the reality of his data and the validity with which he interprets them. As T. S. Eliot remarks of some elements in the novels of Charles Williams, they "are there just because they belonged to the world he lived in, and he could not have kept them out." Thus, whatever is in the life of man is material for the artist. At least one part of the critic's task is to appraise the validity and the implications of the image of man projected by the artist's use of his materials.

Edmund Fuller

Kent, Connecticut
November, 1957

MAN IN MODERN FICTION

*Some Minority Opinions
on Contemporary
American Writing*

Three images of man

Our time has been described variously as an age of
anxiety, an age of schism in the soul, a time when man
suffers not only from war, persecution, famine, and
ruin but from inner problems fully as terrible: despair,
a conviction of isolation, randomness, meaninglessness
in his very existence. The despair, strangely, and the
conviction of meaninglessness, appear to afflict him
most not under conditions of war, persecution, famine, and ruin but under circumstances of material
prosperity and plenty.

There were times, in this century and the previous
one, when the disintegration of society was a major
theme of the writer. Today it is the disintegration of
the individual creature himself—of man. There is no
doubt that in much of our violent, distorted, degraded
fiction a vast, pity-compelling pain and agony are reflected, but the reality of the torment or confusion
from which these creations spring does not insure the
reality of the images of life which they project. The

pity, the compassion, we may feel for either the external or internal sources of these wretched portrayals of life cannot lead us to accept them as valid. Neither can the sincerity of emotion and idea, or the authentic artistic talent that may accompany them, lend validity to partial or distorted images of man and his life.

It is strange how many of the contemporary portrayals of man's suffering are loveless. In many of our novels man's plight and condition are viewed with a chilling detachment. The writers are standing back and looking on either morbidly or indifferently, without either involvement or intervention, after the manner of crowds on a city curb when an accident has happened.

Sometimes actual and active horror are present, sometimes the vestigial traces of a moral revulsion are seen. These are easily repressed, however, in the absence of an authentically responsive love for the human species. Much of the picture of man projected in our fiction is the obvious product of despairing self-hatred, extended from the individual self to the whole race of man, with its accompanying will to degradation and humiliation. It is a clinical condition.

It is obvious, natural, and valuable that the characteristic conditions of an era find reflection in its arts. But that generalization is not enough to explain the form or channels through which the reflection is projected. This chapter is concerned with a theory of origin, or root, for some of our most conspicuous literary symptoms. It is a necessary prologue, by way of definition, to the further examination of characteristics in current fiction with which the rest of the book is occupied.

In the channels of criticism and review there is a good deal of talk, pro or con, about our novelists' preoccupation with despair, brutality, violence, sadism, degeneracy, or merely old-fashioned lust (which is almost considered naïve, now), but there have not been enough attempts to evaluate the precise sources or conditions out of which these strong streams in contemporary writing flow.

Our fiction, in the novels of some of its most touted practitioners, has made a distinct break with the great literary tradition, a break which scarcely has been noted amid the flurry of sales, suppressions, and awards. The question best calculated to place the writer of fiction in one or another of the camps of thought that are so numerous and at such odds today is "What is your view of man?" The answer will place a writer in one of two major folds which are distinct from one another, although within each of them there are numerous subdivisions or secondary categories.

This division which I am seeking to establish certainly has been discernible throughout the long history of human culture, but I think it has never existed on a more critical and decisive scale than in the last century, and especially the last half-century. This division is not clearly recognized in most contemporary criticism, yet I think it holds the key to the comprehension of many phenomena which perplex, pain, or offend the reader of modern fiction.

From some answers to the question "What is your

view of man?" certainly come clues to the cults of violence, brutality, and sexuality, the moods of morbid self-hate, the ache of anxiety and the smothering conviction of isolation and meaninglessness. Man always is the subject of the storyteller, even when he pretends to be writing about imaginary beings or non-humans, as in animal fables, fairy tales, or science-fiction. It is on the nature of man that the world stands divided, for it is out of conflicting views of man and the resultant implications as to how he may be dealt with that radical divisions of a political and economic order arise. On this question men are separated into factions involving politics, ideas, art, science, religion, or any other of the various areas in which we observe that man is divided against himself.

Fundamentally, notwithstanding all the other aspects involved, this is a religious division, for it simply is not possible to express a doctrine about the nature of man without a religious implication of one sort or another.

This world division, of course, does not line up on a simple pattern of countries arrayed against one another. Actually, it cuts across all other lines, and there are specific divisions about the nature of man within the United States, just as there is a general division on this subject between the United States and Russia.

One side of the great division, however subdivided as to creed, sect, or other special premise, holds a view of man that conforms to one expression or another of an unbroken tradition in Western man's history. The other side is singular in the fact that although now of great force and numbers, it takes a position which never before has been accepted as a conscious view by such large numbers of people, even though it has been held by individuals and groups here and there.

Inescapably our literature and other arts reflect these divisions about the nature of man, and where they are not understood, there is difficulty or bewilderment in appraising the reflections in fiction of these conflicts in the minds of men about themselves, their nature, their potentialities, their limitations, their origins, their objectives, and, perhaps above all, their obligations.

All fiction is a comment upon the life and nature of man—though not necessarily consciously so. It cannot help being such inasmuch as varying concepts and projections of the nature of man are the subject of all literature. The writer cannot be wholly coherent, as artist, unless he possesses a wholly coherent view of man to inform, illuminate, and integrate his work.

In other words, every man's novel may not have a *thesis*, but it must have a *premise*—whether declared or tacit, whether conscious or unconscious, it cannot help having a premise. That premise is susceptible to being found out even, as it were, over the author's dead body, and identification of the premise is essential to an evaluation of the work. Explicitly or implicitly, every novel reflects an opinion about the nature of man, even if the author hadn't known he had one.

With exceptions so rare as to be noteworthy, always representing some highly special phenomenon, the vast body of literature from the Hebrews and

Homer down to the early part of the present century, or the latter part of the nineteenth century, has been based upon the tacit or declared premise that there is a God. Sometimes it has been gods—a whole pantheon —as in the pagan tradition. It may have been the God of the Jews, or the Trinitarian God of the Christians, or the Allah of Islam, or the gods of Asia, or those of the Teutons and the Nordics. But whatever, or wher- ever, or however—this vast, centuries-old accretion of our literary heritage is based on the premise that there is a God.

The attitudes of individual writers in relation to God have been infinitely various, even within Holy Scripture. He has been adored, revered, loved, feared, hated, denounced, defied, or denied in the special sense that is in itself religious. He may have been criticized, concepts of Him set at variance with other concepts, but the persistent concept of God dominates the great heritage of our culture.

The appearance of individual strains of thought tending to challenge the very existence of God goes back a long way. But such a challenge has not at- tempted to dominate an entire culture until quite re- cent times. Our present generations now practicing the art of fiction are the first generations in which there have been large, influential, and admired groups of novelists working, in many instances quite uncon- sciously, on the tacit or declared premise that there is no God, basing the patterns of their work on the im- plications, again often unconscious, that arise out of that premise.

Now how does this involve one's view of man? It is possible to forget that the question of whether or not there is a God, with further questions of man's possible relationship with Him, carry incalculable implications about the nature of man and the condition of his life. Also, the writer who does not believe in God, or is indifferent to the question of His existence, may subscribe to the classic Western tradition of man without reflecting upon the premise which is the foundation of this conception. More seriously, the writer who has dismissed or overlooked the relationship between man and God, may find himself projecting an image of the human creature drastically at variance with Western tradition, while either conscious or unconscious that the altered image is the consequence of an altered premise.

In both the Judeo-Christian and Hellenic traditions there is a basic view of man which for all the religiously crucial differences of creed involved still can be reduced to certain premises common to these traditions. In effect, in Western culture they have fused into one tradition.

Within this Western historical-literary tradition, then, man is seen as, or tacitly understood to be, a created being, with an actual or potential relationship to his Creator. Each man is a unique person. Man is seen as inherently imperfect, but with immense possibilities for redemption and reconciliation with his Creator. On the one hand, he is not able to perfect himself through his own works, and the theme of tragedy frequently is his fall through pride in attempting to do so. On the other hand, he is never deterministically fixed in any one state or condition—a point which sufficiently deep reading will substantiate even within the concept of Fate in Greek tragedy. Man is not portrayed as *either* good *or* bad, but as *both* good *and* bad. He inhabits an orderly universe. His fundamental moral laws are commands of his Creator, not just social contracts between himself and his fellows; they are fixed obligations to his God. Thus man, so seen within this vast, varied, but basically consistent tradition, is individual, responsible, guilty, redeemable. Happily, some of the best novels of today still are being written within this great tradition and view of man.

By contrast, we began to find in the last part of the nineteenth century, and then in our own, in great quantity with considerable weight of prestige attached to it, a type of novel the counterpart of which is not to be found, in any significant numbers, earlier than late nineteenth century. It is the work, in many instances, of writers who do not know the implications of what they have written, who are not the architects of their own idea-structures, who are not consciously the mouthpieces of the thesis to which their work is linked.

I speak of the novel of MAN—in capital letters. It is based on the concept of man as a being who is any or all of the following: biologically accidental, self-sufficient, inherently good, ever-progressing, self-perfectible, morally answerable only to his social contracts. He inhabits a morally neutral universe created by random forces. You should recognize this man, for he walks through the pages of many twentieth-century novels and plays. Shaw and Wells were among those who got the movement started. In the most advanced cases, again with some still current, man is identified with God Himself—either collectively in a pantheism, or in the Shavian-Bergsonian view of an emergent, creative-evolutionary God, in whose development man is the growing tip.

But this view already is obsolete and now is over-shadowed by a corollary, or reverse face of the same coin. The last twenty-five years have not been kind to the "better-and-better," inherently good, self-sufficient, emergent-God concepts of man. These have been hard-pushed, even though they are persistent. But some wings of their adherents have broken and given ground. When that optimistic concept of self-generating and progressing man becomes disillusioned or gives way to despair, often an ugly and sinister image emerges which is recognizably from the same root.

From this disillusionment we get that terrible spate of novels now current in which man is seen specifically and insistently as an ironic biological accident, inadequate, aimless, meaningless, isolated, inherently evil, thwarted, self-corrupting, morally answerable to no one, clasped in the vise of determinisms economic or biological. His uniqueness as person is denied or suppressed. He inhabits a hostile universe which is the creation of irrational and possibly malignant forces. The themes of these novels, to borrow some words from Lewis Carroll, are *ambition, distraction, uglification,* and *derision.* Unlike the great tradition of man as individual, responsible, guilty, but redeemable, this despairing disillusionment sees man as collective, irresponsible, morally neuter, and beyond help.

This creature is substantially *less* than true man, *less* than a person. A prime example, Meursault, in Camus' *The Stranger,* is essentially subhuman, whether Camus conceives him as inherently such, or as reduced to such. The same can be said of Nelson Algren's Dove Linkhorn, in *A Walk on the Wild Side,* and a host of figures in other recent American novels.

James Jones' second novel, *Some Came Running,* is characteristic of those that offer us the Yahoo as social arbiter. When Swift created his Yahoos he loathed them as a projection of the subhuman in man. Jones creates Yahoos and has an abiding tenderness for them. One of them he passes off as the type of the artist-writer. His Dave Hirsh, vulgar, often sullen, lecherous, semi-literate as presented to us although supposed to be sensitive and gifted to the point of near genius, is a specimen of the Yahoo-hero of the tough novelists. This person's values, credos, standards, and tastes are generalized into those of the writer in the abstract. His are the social and human-value judgments in which this novel and so many like it see the world. He is moderator of the Jonesian Forum.

Through this mouthpiece, Jones states an aim for the writer and a specific view of man. Dave aspires to

> force the human race for once to take an un-
> varnished unsugarcoated look at itself for a
> change. . . . They would recoil in such shock
> and horror at themselves that foreverafter
> never again would the name of D. HIRSH
> be mentioned in polite society.

Dave reflects upon Thoreau's "Most men lead lives
of quiet desperation," and amends it to "Most men
lead lives of desperate crappiness." Pursuing this theme,
with his familiar grace of style, he broods:

> There had been so much crap written about
> the greatness of humanity and love for the
> human race it like to turned your stomach. It
> was about time somebody did a little expos-
> ing. . . . He wanted to write the truth about
> life. The real truth. Not all that crap that
> sentimental jerks crammed together into novels
> and tried to pretend was literature. The *real*
> truth about life as it was *really* lived.

We are asked by such literary levelers (always
leveling *down*, as Johnson observed) to accept this
alleged truth, these judgments, standards, and visions
of life, either in the name of a pseudo compassion or
of a pseudo democracy. We must accept the spreading cult of semi-literacy of which Dave is a voice.
Man is a failure and a fraud. The Yahoo must prevail.
To resist him is to be a snob.

There is a substantial body of modern fiction representing this view of man. It is part of what C. S. Lewis
has called *The Abolition of Man* in the brilliant little

book of that name. This view is either still spreading, or else at best has only stopped expanding but is holding its own. What is more, it has the full cry of whole schools of literary critics who have established a canon and an esthetic for it. It includes the atheistical wing of the existentialists, the less consciously intellectual, mere "tough guy," writers, and a few "arty" pornographers.

It is no slight matter when we are asked to give our literary accolades, uncritical of the conceptual contents of the books, to works and writers who tacitly or explicitly deny the freedom and responsibility—in short, the essential manhood—of man. The literary merits of many such touted books are not so extraordinary as to carry them alone—we must assume unless assured otherwise that the total package, implications and all, is being bought by the juries or critics involved. Particularly open to attack on this count are National Book Award juries. In their eight years, so far, they have passed over many titles to demonstrate that you must (almost in alternate years) be either sufficiently degraded in your image of man or sufficiently obscure in style to pull down the award.

Naturally, as in all attempts at general formulation, there are some writers who fall astraddle of the categories I have enumerated, or who oscillate, from book to book or even within the same book, back and forth across their dividing lines. We can recognize a category of what might be called the "God-residue" novel. Some of our ablest craftsmen write it. They may be considered the spokesmen of T. S. Eliot's "decent,

Godless people, whose only monuments are asphalt roads and a thousand lost golf balls."

I think the term "God-residue" is quite precise. In general such writers are sensitive, gifted, ethical humanists. They think that the only thing wrong with religion is the naïve idea of God. They think, reluctantly, that God does not exist but that it would be well for men to live as if He did. But "as if" is not a sound foundation for construction or creation. The literature which these writers produce may be competent, but often is singularly impotent. They are at their best, inevitably, with the presently outdated social or sociological novel, the "liberal" novel, or the "case-history" novel. There are able storytellers among the "God-residue" people, yet much of their literature is withering on the vine, often portraying a waning political effectiveness, or crumbling psychic structures, in the present arena of clashing ideas. I fear that they are dry bones in the valley of decision. They are marooned on "maybe so" while "yes" and "no" are at war about the basic nature of man.

A writer cannot be required to believe in God, or to accept a specific theology if he does believe. We may rejoice when a writer emerges who is intelligently affirmative about the human enterprise, but we cannot demand affirmation, like the prophets of "positive thinking." We are limited to analyzing and appraising the vision each writer offers us.

Whether believing or disbelieving in a God standing in a personal relationship to man, there have been some writers, always, speaking as a minority voice

within the great Western tradition of man. The function of such writers—and it is a valuable one—is to
ask the anguished questions which life ever demands
of the thinking man, believer or skeptic. Many such
writers are peculiarly conscious of the gap between
human pretension and reality. Not offering a view
of man counter to, or in challenge of, the Judeo-Christian Western tradition, nevertheless they are compelled to probe and test unsparingly the validity of that
tradition. They are disquieting, and it is needful for
man to be disquieted, particularly in periods when
complacency, or conformity, produces stagnation at
one extreme wing of our culture, while repudiation
of the whole human enterprise is aggressively vocal
at the other.

I believe the late George Orwell was such a prober,
who felt the dilemma of his position with a peculiar
intensity. He was firm in what he rejected but uncertain of what he accepted. He wished to preserve, but
had become profoundly skeptical of, the Western tradition of man. His skepticism had driven him close to
the Marxist image of man. The depth of his pessimism
in *1984* lay in the fact that if man is as the Marxist
contends him to be, the equivalent of the society of
1984 is logical and inevitable in his future. He hoped to
warn us away from such a future, but was not greatly
hopeful that the warning could avert it.

A deep skepticism about the human enterprise per-
vades James Gould Cozzens' *By Love Possessed*. I think
the relief of receiving this brilliantly controlled, mature
work of craftsmanship in the midst of the deluge of

fictional slop may have caused many readers to fail to perceive its reservations about the human creature. This element markedly defines or limits the kind of impact the novel has. *By Love Possessed* interests intellectually, fascinates, and evokes admiration for its mastery of technique, but it does not move us deeply or stir the emotions powerfully. We are not intimately involved. It is written with detachment and read with detachment.

The atheistical wing of the existentialists asserts the meaninglessness of life and the primacy of death. Nicholas Berdyaev answers this with the affirmation that "Deeper truth lies in the fact that the world is not meaningless and absurd, but is in a meaningless state." The definition of that state, the tragedy of it, the origin of it, and the refusal of it are the greatest themes available to the writer today.

Paul Tillich has said that "Man is that being who asks the question of being." This is the true existentialism, for whatever that dismal term is worth. The irony is that the atheistical existentialists, vainly trying to ask the question of being while engaged in negating it, should think that a creature capable of conceiving and attacking so awesome and self-conscious a question could be a creature of random origin and meaningless life.

In the chapters that follow, I am criticizing, in terms of the image of man, a number of contemporary books and their writers. Even in doing so, I recognize that there is no use in inveighing against the artist for what he sees. The writer can only portray the world he sees, and so *must* portray it. Yet we can ask profitably what sometimes causes him to see only a distorted world, or a debased human image. The critical appraisal of his stature and validity as an artist is immediately involved. The possible sickness, lostness, or purblindness of the writer himself are qualifiers of his worth. Yet they do not not negate his worth entirely —the nature of man being what it is.

The honest writer should recognize what some writers in some eras have refused to face—that any degradation is possible to a free creature of God. He should recognize also what some of our present writers refuse to face—that no degradation can be ultimate or definitive for this same creature. There is no path down without a path up, there is also no height without its inviting abyss. The path may sometimes be the same, with up or down a question of direction of travel.

My own conception of the image of man, and of the writer's great theme, is well expressed in some words of Stephen F. Bayne, to whom the great sense of writing and reading alike is "that we may see man as he is, single and whole, reasoning and choosing and believing, half of this world and half of some other, the only animal who must decide what kind of animal he will be, the only beast it is shameful to call a beast, whose soul, as Boethius said, 'albeit in a cloudy memory, yet seeks back his own good, but like a drunken man knows not the way home.' "

I believe that all the strands of contemporary fiction can be subsumed and understood in their origin and motivation under the above views of man. Most important, I believe that in the curdled disillusionment of the worship of the creature instead of the Creator we find the source of the ugliest, most loveless and despairing, veins of modern writing. I think, too, that the prevailing trend is shifting, and that a renewed literature in the great tradition of man as a rational, free, responsible, purposeful—even though fallible and imperfect—creature of God is emerging. Evil in all its range will not disappear from his portrayal, for this very man is inextricably compounded of elements of good and evil, but we will no longer be given the illusion that the seamy aspect of man is the sum total of man, which is the distortion in so much current writing. We are restoring the vitally dramatic picture of what Martin Buber has called "the hell-tormented and heaven-storming generations of men."

2

The revival of total depravity

Calvin brought to the Christian teaching about Original Sin and the Fall of Man a dire extremity of interpretation that became known as Total Depravity. All men were seen as steeped utterly in corruption, totally depraved in all their faculties, to be saved only by faith in the redeeming grace of Christ. In marked contrast, the classical catholic doctrine of the nature of man, though regarding man's moral nature as "wounded" by the Fall and also requiring redemption through Christ, never has taught and firmly rejects the idea of man's nature having become totally depraved or intrinsically evil. Vestiges of the Image of God and elements of natural theology and morality are still left in him.

The extreme Calvinist view, of course, twisted even beyond its original implications, was the breeding ground of the stark, bleak, cruel excesses of Puritanism, which, while condemning all impulses of the human heart and mind, also returned to that strain of dualistic Manicheanism that has dogged Christian history, and pronounced the body, the flesh, and all that beautified or gratified it, to be corrupt and evil. This is not, and never was, Christianity, but is one of those divergent blunders from it to which even those who most devoutly profess it remain liable.

Our age sees much discussion of Christianity based on erroneous conceptions. This is nowhere more true than in the case of the doctrine of Original Sin. The liberal humanist who often does not know what that doctrine is but doesn't care for the sound of it ("sin" is not a popular word), conceives it as a harsh and unjust teaching. My own experience of it has been quite the opposite. It has, in my own simple vernacular, brought me immense relief by helping me to understand why I'm persistently cussed and perverse when I don't intend to be. St. Paul put it more gracefully when he said, "For I do not do what I want, but I do the very thing I hate." What Freud called the id is Original Sin. Understood in Christianity the doctrine is humane and releases man, as he is, from the burden of feeling that he should have attained a perfection which is, by his circumstances, impossible to him. No one is crueler than he who would exhort man, as he is, to become perfect. Christ's "You, therefore, must be perfect," like the rest of the Sermon on the Mount, is the revelation of the law of the Kingdom of God, not of the kingdom of this earth, to which it stands both as beacon and rebuke.

The Judeo-Christian man is a free man. The enemy of free man is determinism, of any kind. There was much determinism in the Greek concept of Fate, but even this was not total. It is not simply a matter of the foreseeing prophecy; it is also in the particular characters of individual tragic heroes to act in such a way as to fulfill the prophecy and thus compound their doom. But the Calvinistic doctrine of the elect and the non-elect is wholly deterministic. Marxism-Leninism is deterministic, looking toward the perfection of man after the dictatorship of the proletariat. Some have made of those great clinical insights opened by Freud a determinism which, properly understood, they are not. But perhaps no group, outside of party-line organizations, has so espoused determinism as certain contemporary novelists.

The shallow, case-history method of characterization, often the result of ill-digested Freudian ideas, tends to present pictures of trapped creatures, boxed creatures, possessing no freedom of choice or movement whatever because of some determining, traumatic event, triumphantly disclosed by the writer at his chosen moment. Because of *this* the person has become *that*. The case-history device fails because it presumes to be complete, whereas no explanation or exposition of character ever can be complete in art or in life. We never know *all* the facts. The presumption of completeness, thus, is what introduces the falseness in such character delineations.

The theme of "No Exit" (Sartre), of the creature with no way out, is prominent among us. A true view of man, a fully human view, never finds man wholly without choice. Yes, the life of man, circumstantially, environmentally, economically, or morally can bring him, sometimes with appalling abruptness, to points of extremely limited choice. But he has always the choice of yes or no, in the sense of moral consent, so long as he is rational. When he is irrational, and no longer morally free, this is either medically or circumstantially accidental, or possibly the end result, the checkmate, from his own previous choices. If he be a condemned man, justly or unjustly, he may have no further choice whether to live or die, but there remains the choice of how to accept the death. Choice, or decision, is the glory of man and the burden of man. Contrary to our common slogans, it is not a freedom which man always welcomes, as Dostoevsky definitively set forth in "The Grand Inquisitor."

A concept of man that views him as not possessing these elements of freedom and self-determination is a concept of something less than man, essentially sub-human—the unman. One can, in a manner of speaking, dehumanize oneself, embrace the state of unman, enter the Wasteland, by waiving, negating, rejecting, or denying the endowment of free will and moral re-sponsibility. This is truly to resign from the human race. Or, in the case of barbarous, taboo-and-totem-ridden primitives, it is not to have ascended as yet to the full human state. Totem and taboo, of course, in various forms, are still much with us even in our most advanced and complex cultures.

The most terrifying thing depicted in much fiction is blind, uninterpreted, meaningless, causeless corrup-tion and malignancy. These qualities are offered to us as simply existential—they just *are*. Either they are taken as pure evil, or else worse, the very idea of evilness is dismissed and only beingness of this sort is acknowledged.

The Christian doctrine of man knows no such thing as pure evil. In the Christian tradition, evil is only a good gone wrong, turned aside, misused, missing its mark, wrongly chosen. It has no absoluteness of its own, nor has it a permanence other than the duration given it by continuation of the original wrong choice, or its results. Evil can stop, or can be transmuted and redeemed, within any specific context of its occurrence, though it cannot disappear from the experience of man, because man is wounded by having placed himself in a context of partial alienation from his Creator and from the original state intended for him. This is a part of Christian teaching.

If, because I am writing frankly from a Christian premise, it seems to anyone that I insist too much upon the Christian doctrine of man, remember that this is essentially Western civilization's doctrine of man. It is essentially the Jewish view of man. It is preponderantly harmonious with important aspects of the Greek view, in which much of man's sorrow stems from offense against the gods, and in which pride is the greatest sin. The doctrine of man which I am expounding has shaped the thought of the greatest minds of Western culture throughout its history, and it has sharpened the sensitivities to our human condition for all the great masters of literature in all the European languages and in English. The non-Christian humanist is the inheritor of this same doctrine, which he has simply stripped of its Cause or Creator.

Some modern writers, like certain characters in Dostoevsky, believe in the Devil but not in God. Some believe in God but not in the Devil. Some believe in neither God nor the Devil. The great problem is—if one rejects the Judeo-Christian, Western-civilization tradition of the nature of man, how does one explain evil? Some, as I have said, do not explain it but present it with either no comment or intended implication, or present it more consciously as the existential "given-ness" of the human situation, having no origin or reason, but simply being. Dorothy Sayers has said, "Humanism is always apt to underestimate, and to be baffled by, the deliberate will to evil."

Two American writers, feeling a compulsion with which I must say I am sympathetic, to find a reason for evil, have put forward two remarkably strange views. They are in that now disillusioned camp that had wished to see man as inherently good, but having been compelled by their own honesty and perceptiveness to perceive the reality of evil in their world, tried to improvise an explanation for it, rather than accept the classical doctrine I have been discussing. As a result, they have come up with an unwitting revival of a Calvinist doctrine—Total Depravity. I find this to be one of the choice ironies of our literature.

I have in mind John Steinbeck, in *East of Eden,* and William March, in *The Bad Seed,* both books having met with a wide popular acceptance.

Mr. Steinbeck has created for us Cathy Ames, a

perverse and evil child, who begins by committing numerous childish sex offenses, advances to burning her parents to death, and marches on to become whore and madam-extraordinary. Cathy is evil. Mr. Steinbeck agrees, remarking that "there was a time when a girl like Cathy would have been called possessed by the devil," but he will not call her so. He has an explanation of his own:

> I believe there are monsters born in the world to human parents. Some you can see, misshapen and horrible, with huge heads or tiny bodies; some are born with no arms, no legs, some with three arms, some with tails or mouths in odd places. They are accidents and no one's fault, as used to be thought. Once they were considered the visible punishments for concealed sins.
>
> And just as there are physical monsters, can there not be mental or psychic monsters born? The face and body may be perfect, but if a twisted gene or a malformed egg can produce physical monsters, may not the same process produce a malformed soul?
>
> Monsters are variations from the accepted normal to a greater or less degree. As a child may be born without an arm, so one may be born without kindness or the potential of conscience. . . .
>
> It is my belief that Cathy Ames was born with the tendencies, or lack of them, which drove and forced her all of her life. Some balance wheel was misweighted, some gear out of ratio. She was not like other people, never was from birth. . . .

Here we have Steinbeck's full case for Cathy. Now what of William March's Rhoda Penmark? We find the identical monster theory: "some inborn, pre-destined thing . . . they were the true, inborn criminals that can neither be changed nor modified. . . ." But where Steinbeck had predicated the occurrence of the type as random, March made it hereditary. Rhoda is totally depraved because her maternal grandmother had been totally depraved; it is a genetic flaw, and the mother sees herself as the intermediary who "carried the bad seed that made her what she is." This is a fantastic genetic gobbledygook, in addition to being a ridiculous conception of the moral nature of man.

Something approaching this, but not as clearly defined, occurred in the 1930s in Lillian Hellman's play *The Children's Hour*, in which little Mary Tilford was projected as a child of preternatural malignancy, "A strange girl, a bad girl. There's something very awful the matter with her." Miss Hellman, however, stayed essentially within the possibility of a mentally sick child without the elaborate character theories of Steinbeck and March.

What these gentlemen have done in these two books, unbeknownst to themselves, is to revive a variant of Calvin's Total Depravity. But how much more ruthless and cruel in their implications are the ideas of Steinbeck and March in this instance. The total depravity of Cathy and Rhoda, instead of at least placing them in the same condition as all men, has instead set them utterly apart from all men. Whereas Calvin set forth at least the hope of redemption through faith for some of his totally depraved (among whom he numbered himself), what redemption or hope of body or spirit is there for the monsters, Cathy and Rhoda, so carefully defined as hideous jokes or freaks of a blind genetic accident? Steinbeck's and March's concept of character and destiny in these two books is the most cruel I have encountered in contemporary fiction.

In March's case, because of the superficial and contrived structure of the entire story, it simply means that the novel, and Maxwell Anderson's play adapted from it, have no vestige of value other than as artificial melodrama. The inherent ludicrousness of the basic concept was highlighted by the lightning stroke from a presumably wrathful God inserted at the end by Hollywood to bring the necessary moral comeuppance as the movies understand such things.

In Steinbeck's case, Cathy Ames is a faulty thread, a weakness of concept and character grasp, seriously marring what is, in some other respects, one of his most substantial and thoughtful books, in a class apart from the meretricious slop of his *Cannery Row-Sweet Thursday* mood. The effect of his monster thesis is to render meaningless the elaborately drawn lifelong portrait of Cathy. She can have no moral significance or identification value if she is a random mutant, a moral freak. By his precise definition, she is inhuman, a female of the subspecies unman.

Running through these books, and many others, is a more subtle and sophisticated, yet still discernible classification of people into the good guys and the bad guys. A deeper view of man, as creature, is needed.

Man is not either good or bad; he is both good and bad. Curiously, I think the failure to see the badness in good does more to distort character understanding than failure to see the goodness in bad. With a shallow doctrine of man as basis, it is then the failure to see the bad intermingled with good that leads to disillusionment and cynicism. If an excessive, sentimental idealism or perfectionism about man exists, the almost inevitable disillusionment of this easily leads to a sweeping bitterness and the assertion that everything is rotten. If the idealized woman image proves unfaithful, then *all* women are unfaithful. If the idealized male image is discovered to be dishonest, then *all* men are dishonest. The popular song is the great simplification of this principle; the torch singer sings of the faithlessness of all men or all women because of the man or woman who has betrayed. It is our weakness that when we discover bad in good we are much more apt to generalize sweepingly about it than when we discover good in bad. It is easier to hate than to love, easier to reject than to accept.

The complex view of man has not vanished from the contemporary novel. In his best book to date, *The Spiral Road*, Jan de Hartog presents a number of richly realized characters in the total blend of elements that are man. Most appropriate to this thesis, however, is the study of Betsy and Willem Watereus. Betsy was a whore in the slums of Amsterdam and Willem was a thief. Mr. de Hartog leads them along a long road (not even the central road of his novel) to that condition which we sometimes call sainthood. This is not done in sentimental generalizations, but through agony. He never shows us a time when either of this pair "has it made," in the current vernacular, but shows the endless tension of choice and decision along the whole way. The historic annals of sainthood contain many progressions from one condition to another that are as striking, and document the fact that the contest is never finished. Perhaps one of the chief points to emphasize is that unlike so many of the portrayers of degradation, de Hartog has not left his characters just where he picked them up, but has carried them through transitions that disclose the full range of man.

Don't suppose that I insist that transitions be always upward. There are classical types of the downward movement. I think of George Hurstwood, in *Sister Carrie*. There is also the downward swing with the suggested potential of redemption, as in Raskolnikov, or Pieter van Vlanderen in Paton's *Too Late the Phalarope*. It is also the unquestioned right of the novelist to show a man down and leave him down. My desire, in such case, is to see it in a context that is clearly particular, not tacitly universal. A good example, in a varied and broad context, is Gertrude, the sister of Stephen Kumalo, in *Cry, the Beloved Country*, who was unable to shake off the pattern of her deteriorated life.

In a rather remarkable first novel, *The Eighth Day*, Robert C. Goldston has used the figure of an insane murderer and made of this image of disaster an instrument of the grace of God. This is worth remark on my premise of the Christian doctrine of man, for its abandonment has led not only to writers failing to recognize the full scope of what man is and can be and do, but it also overlooks the unlimited capacity of the Creator to use such instrumentalities as He will. Holy Scripture and the lives of the saints make it quite clear that He does not rely upon the respectable.

3

The new compassion in the American novel

Never a glycerin tear shed to the tune of "Hearts and Flowers" in a Victorian tear-jerker was so sloppy and false as is the weird sentimentality in some of the roughest and supposedly most "realistic" of modern novels. An inverted pathos has sprung up among what Maxwell Geismar has called "the brutes." For some years, authors, publishers and reviewers have kicked around the word *compassion* so loosely that its meaning may become corrupted and lost.

The present decline of compassion (which also is the decline of tragedy) began in an odd and relatively innocuous way. It started with the vogue of the lovable bums, and at first it was no worse than a foolish romanticizing of the scalawag: a beery, brass-rail sentimentality. This pattern was not completely new—we see a bit of it in all the classical picaros—but never had it been so elaborated as it began to be in the thirties. It had charm and appeal, at times, dealing good-naturedly with human foibles. It is possible to look affectionately upon such people, as with Wilkins Micawber, if you keep your head and don't elevate a mood into a philosophy.

Some writers, especially those talented men William Saroyan, in *The Time of Your Life*, and John Steinbeck, in several books from his early *Tortilla Flat* to his recent *Sweet Thursday*, developed the lovable bums into the fallacy of "the beautiful little people"—which almost always meant the shiftless, the drunk, the amoral, and the wards of society. A corollary was implied: if you didn't love these characters, you were a self-righteous bigot, hard of heart by contrast to the author's compassion and love for the common clay of humanity. Conversely, these books imply another world of respectable and economically stable people who vaguely are not nice, not right, compared to the ineffable and intransigent "little people."

Yet some, though not all, of this stuff called itself "realistic." Its absurdities reached a point in Steinbeck's *The Wayward Bus*, which inspired John Mason Brown to one of the most searching remarks since the little boy said the emperor wasn't wearing any clothes: "If realism isn't real, then isn't it trash?"

A sinister twist came in the path some years ago, and abruptly this new soft streak lost its innocence. The lovable bum began to slip away, and in his place emerged the genial rapist, the jolly slasher, the fun-loving dope pusher. Now we see increasingly a technique of simple identification with the degraded which is miscalled compassion. It lacks the requisites for compassion as much as its subjects lack the requisites for tragedy.

What is compassion, anyhow? It means the sharing of a sorrow, a pity and sympathy, a desire to help—feeling another's pain or plight as if it were one's own, seeing "those in chains as bound with them." It applies to a man's moral as well as material or physical breakdown. In the moral realm it recognizes the sharing of all human guilt, the potentiality of evil in the most blameless, the element which the Christian calls Original Sin and the analyst calls the id. In the traditions of both tragic and pathetic literature there is an abundance of authentic compassion.

A large and generous view of life and a distinct standard of values are necessary to establish compassion. These need not, of course, be formulated, but at least you must be able to discriminate between a happy state and an unhappy one; you must be able to discern the difference between a man destroyed through his own fault and one destroyed through no fault of his own, with all the delicate gradations possible between. You must set a moral value on man's actions and circumstances. Compassion is not a suspension of judgment, it is a judgment tempered and chastened according to the facts under some definable theory of the human condition. Compassion is discernment of the gap between the man that is and the potential man that was.

Two old saws contain much of the truth about the compassionate view of life and, incidentally, remove its unavoidable judgments from any taint of smugness: "There but for the grace of God go I" and "To understand all is to forgive all." How these apply to the phony compassion in many current novels we shall see.

In the enthusiastic critical reception of *From Here to Eternity*, culminating in the National Book Award, the word *compassion* was sprayed all over the scene by the critical fraternity. The writing of James Jones may well have many admirable attributes, but I do not see wherein compassion is one of them.

Like all the other pseudo-tough young writers engaged in this peculiar transposition of values, Mr. Jones is shamelessly and laughably sentimental. This is missed by some simply because he isn't sentimental about Mother or Dad or the Pure Girl or Jesus or Darling Babies. Instead, he is sentimental about in- corrigible anti-social and criminal types and whores. He is said to be compassionate toward these—which is as you choose to think. Certainly, though, if you are *not* one of these you may expect short shrift from Mr. Jones, for he has precious little compassion for any- one else.

If you can wipe Mr. Jones' tears out of your eyes, you will see that the famous Private Robert E. Lee Prewitt is not a social being, nor are his buddies. Pre- witt is not the most extreme of them, but he is the "hero." His type is a social hazard. Since many men have endured as much in the way of background ex- perience as Prewitt did, he is no more the helpless crea- tion of something outside him than anyone else. His character is partly, even largely, self-created, as is true, for practical purposes, of most of us.

But, says Compassionate Jones: Prewitt, Maggio,

Stark and the others, drinking and whoring, knifing and slugging, rolling homosexuals, defying authority indiscriminately and eternally, are good, good people. All authority, all sobriety, all the rest of the world, are bad. He is vindictive against the socially adjusted or constructive. If you listen to him long you'll be ashamed to be sober and out of jail. This is not compassion; it is paranoia.

And this is why some of us regard *From Here to Eternity* not as a controlled work of art but as a clinically interesting projection of personalities by a man endowed with genuine gifts for narrative and pictorial characterization. Whether we are right or wrong, the minority holding this opinion must state it, in the face of reviews, sales and awards.

The most interesting case I've seen since Jones is a first novel of some seasons ago by George Mandel, *Flee the Angry Strangers*. It made no special mark in hard covers, though circulated widely in paper reprint. I choose it as a peculiarly apt illustration of a tendency which can be demonstrated in variations in many novels. In it the false compassion takes the ever more common form of complete negation of values and denial of responsibility. The author's interpreter, in the book, looks on the world of dope addiction and shrugs away any helpful intervention on these grounds: "Who the hell am I to stop it? Who am I to decide about people? There's no harm in anything. You can't stop any of that. You have no right. Nobody has."

With this view, he concludes that all the fallen are

the result of repressive nay-saying by the unfallen. (Why the unfallen didn't fall is never explained.) And again emerges the teary slobbering over the criminal and degraded, the refusal to assign any share of responsibility to them, and a vindictive lashing out against the rest of the world.

This particular "compassion" is the sentimental pretense that things are not what they are. Mr. Mandel's eighteen-year-old heroine, addicted to drugs, sexually delinquent, mother of an illegitimate child, finally has been put in an institution. Mr. Mandel supports her in the outraged lament, "My own mother put me there."

As this girl escapes, steps up the dope, takes on more men indiscriminately, and tries a little prostitution, she can still say, reproachfully, "You think I'm a tramp."

"Shucks, kid," is the general attitude of the new-compassion boys, "just going around and doing everything a tramp does, doesn't make a good, sweet, clean little kid like you a tramp."

In short, the new compassion is the denial that men and women are what their consistent, voluntary (and involuntary) patterns of action make them. The elements of true tragedy and compassion—the fall from a standard, responsibility however extenuated, repentance, and the struggle for rehabilitation—are not in this philosophy.

What is wrong with Mandel's approach to his delinquent heroine? He feels sorry for her—don't we all? Can he deny that she has become a tramp? Compassion is to see precisely what she is (which he evades), analyze how she got that way (which he distorts or oversimplifies), and seek for what can be done to rehabilitate her (which he refuses). This is the weakness of many such novels.

It is no casual matter that authors, publishers, and reviewers should blandly accept such attitudes as compassion. It may be the most unwholesome and dangerous single symptom in modern literature, for as there is nothing more appealing than the cloak of compassion, there is nothing more treacherous when it is false. In literary art, this is the absolute end product of ethical relativism. No valid compassion can exist without a moral framework. The Greeks had such a framework. The Judeo-Christian tradition has one. Only in recent years, in the work of some groups of writers, especially in the French existentialist movement, has the moral framework quietly and completely dropped away. This new compassion is a danger to the art of writing, and a deadly one when it is accepted on its claims.

These writers are trapped in a terrible contradiction. Their form of compassion is not to blame, and they find that they cannot portray life at all without assigning blame. Therefore, since their concept of compassion will not permit them to blame anything upon the criminal, the degraded, and the destroyed, they blame everything upon the non-criminal, the non-degraded and the undestroyed. It is a kind of counter-puritanism.

The irony is that these writers have no intermediate ground. Many so-called good people are responsible for the destruction of others. All of us are involved in the guilt of mankind. Throughout literature and life we see it. But you have to have a standard of values in order to see how corrupt, warped, misdirected values destroy themselves and others. That's the realm of tragedy, of individuality and subtlety. If you have no values, and see no values, you cannot distinguish the hypocrite from the virtuous man, the self-righteous man from the genuinely good, the Uriah Heep from the man of honest humility. The world contains them all, and more. Beginning by seeing only bad, the new compassion ends by inverting it to be a curious "good" to which normal life stands as a kind of "bad." "Evil, be thou my good": this is the key to our paranoid novelists.

The existentialists and those influenced by them, and many who unconsciously have been practicing existentialists without the fancy jargon, portray human depravity and degradation without comment, presumably as they see it. This is a kind of moral neutralism. It makes no judgment, on the grounds that there is no judgment. But these writers show phenomena without meaning. If we give depravity no significance we imply that it has no significance. Far from being neutral or unmoralistic or undogmatic, this is a highly partisan, positive philosophical position indeed.

The conflict between good and evil is a common thread running through all the great literature and drama of the world, from the Greeks to ourselves. The principle that conflict is at the heart of all dramatic action, when illustrated by concrete example, almost always turns up some aspect of the struggle between good and evil.

The idea that there is neither good nor evil—in any absolute moral or religious sense—is widespread in our times. There are various relativistic, behavioristic standards of ethics. If they even admit the distinction between good and evil they see it as a relative matter and not as the whirlwind of choices at the center of living. In any such state of mind, conflict can be only a petty matter at best, lacking true universality. The acts of the evildoer and of the virtuous man alike become dramatically neutralized. Imagine *Crime and Punishment* or *The Brothers Karamazov* if Dostoevsky had thought that the good and the evil in those books were wholly a relative matter and had had no conviction about them.

You can't have a vital literature if you ignore or shun evil. What you get then is the goody-goody in place of the good, the world of Pollyanna. *Cry, the Beloved Country* is a great and dramatic novel because Alan Paton, in addition to his skill of workmanship, sees with clear eyes both good and evil, differentiates them, pitches them into conflict with each other, *and takes sides*. He sees that the native boy, Absalom Kumalo, who has murdered, cannot be judged justly without taking into account the environment that has partly shaped him. But he sees, too, that Absalom the individual, not society the abstraction, did the act and has responsibility. Mr. Paton understands mercy. He knows that this precious thing is not shown on sentimental impulse, but after searching examination of the realities of human action. Mercy follows a judgment; it does not precede it.

One of the novels of the talented Paul Bowles, *Let It Come Down*, is full of motion, full of sensational depravities, and is a crashing bore. For the book recognizes no good, admits no evil, and is coldly indifferent to the moral behavior of its characters. It is a long shrug. Such a view of life is non-dramatic, negating the vital essence of drama.

Charles Jackson is a novelist unmistakably sensitive and gifted. His novels are terrifyingly preoccupied with modes of demoralization and collapse. They depict these faithfully, but take in no other aspects of life at all. He admires and partly emulates Dostoevsky, but he does not appear to realize that the difference between the dark tones of his own work and those in Dostoevsky's novels is precisely that Dostoevsky took sides. He was not neutral in the conflict between good and evil. The gulf fixed between Jackson and Dostoevsky is not one of literary craftsmanship but of moral sense.

Dostoevsky views Raskolnikov with compassion, for he sees and interprets for us the moral fallacy that entrapped Raskolnikov. If there were no such fallacy, if Dostoevsky had perceived no moral standard to be warped, Raskolnikov (whose name means "the dissenter") would have been a mere Russian Robert E. Lee Prewitt, and there would have been no tragedy. The great depth of *Crime and Punishment* (the very title states it) is that both Dostoevsky the author and Raskolnikov the created character are conscious of the moral dilemma.

Dreiser, in *An American Tragedy*, sees Clyde

Griffiths with compassion because he shows us how the boy has been undermined by a shoddy set of material values and is poorly equipped to appraise them. Dreiser sees the good and evil in the American era he portrays; the social tragedy is that there are those like Clyde who can see them only dimly, if at all.

The original muckrakers portrayed horrors with a fierce indignation against the social injustice they saw as causative, if sometimes too simply. So it is in Upton Sinclair's *The Jungle*. But these men were reformers. Their eyes were fixed upon a good of which they saw men deprived, and which they were determined passionately to restore. In the writers we are discussing, the vision of the good is lost. They stare hypnotized upon the mess as if they conceived it to be the sole, or total, reality of life.

Many novelists of talent other than those named are more or less involved in the confusion of identification with compassion, in the process of representing a facet of life as if it were the whole and of presenting phenomena without the evaluation which the greatest of writers, and even the mere reformers, never have shrunk from offering. They feel that by detailing innumerable horrors without visible revulsion they are somehow demonstrating sympathy. They conceive their virtue as not casting stones at the sinner, but many cast stones in other directions, and some reverse the words of Jesus to say, in effect, "Neither do I condemn you—go and sin some more."

National Book Award juries have shown an affinity for new-compassion novels. In addition to *From Here to Eternity*, they have given the palm to Nelson Algren's *The Man with the Golden Arm* and Saul Bellow's *The Adventures of Augie March*. In Algren's skillful work, including the recent *A Walk on the Wild Side*, there may be sympathy, but it remains the one-sided sympathy of the new compassion. The promising talent of Norman Mailer has collapsed utterly into this genre in *Barbary Shore* and *The Deer Park*. Leonard Bishop's novels belong there, and Irving Shulman's at least lean that way. The total catalogue of writers and books within this category would be burdensome to compile.

Some borderline books of the kind we are discussing are no more than crying novels or—to be more blunt about a few—sniveling novels. A vast and blurred self-pity is appliquéd upon the fictional characters—as if to do this represented compassion in the author. In some cases it is simple transference of the author's own self-pity, as shown by the inability to see or move beyond it in portraying life. In some, the assiduous stockpiling of depravities has an unmistakable element of reveling, of wallowing, of bad-boy's glee. Many of these writers cry, "Look, Ma, I'm blaspheming."

There are merely fitful glimmerings of life and agitated motions in the books of such novelists. The vital questions which would bring them to profound life have been nullified. You cannot say of their attitude toward their characters, "To understand all is to forgive all." They see much but understand nothing. They do not understand all—they *devalue* all. They do not forgive all. They do not forgive anything. They say there is nothing to forgive. They take murder, rape, perversion and say, belligerently, "What's wrong with it?"

You cannot say of their characters, "There but for the grace of God go I," because you cannot find in their work any chain of moral cause and effect by which *you* could get from where *you* are to where their characters are (as you can in Dostoevsky and Paton). The placement of these characters in their situations is arbitrary and mechanical, as is the inversion of good and bad.

The irony of ironies is that these are not the most compassionate, but the most vindictive writers working today; not the most humble, but the most arrogant; not the binders of the wounds of their fallen brothers, but the destroyers of the social order. "Down! Down everybody!" they scream. "Down with us all!"

Dostoevsky anticipated this moral phenomenon as he did so many others. These paranoid novels are books that some of his brilliantly studied characters might have written. Ivan Karamazov said, "Everything is permitted," and Smerdyakov, acting accordingly, murdered. Raskolnikov saw moral law as inapplicable to some men, and acting accordingly, murdered. Ideas are more than abstractions, Dostoevsky shows us again and again. Ideas have consequences. God preserve us from the consequences of the ideas implicit in the novels of the new compassion.

4

John Aldridge and the search for values

For some time, now, Mr. John W. Aldridge has been padding up and down the literary byways, like Diogenes, lantern in hand, looking for a heretic. The book, *In Search of Heresy*, voices his cry that all he can find is conformity. As a result, he has been driven to a do-it-yourself heresy, himself cast as the heretic within the "conformist values of our new mass culture."

His earlier book, *After the Lost Generation*, lamented the absence of values and saw in this the dilemma of the generation of post-World-War-II writers. His general theories about writers—the conditions of their work, and why they respond to their time as they do—seem blurred. He would have it that the "lost generation" of the Dos Passos, Hemingway, Fitzgerald era was lost because its inherited structure of values had collapsed. Its one advantage lay in having witnessed the collapse and being able to dramatize it. The later generations couldn't lose these values all over again, for they had never been regained. All that was left for them to do, therefore, was to dramatize war itself, and when that was over, certain "newly discovered" areas of subject matter, such as homosexuality and racial conflicts. Since propounding these views he has come to see the writer cramped and inhibited by a vast wave of conformity to mass values. He stomps on the prostrate bodies of Sloan Wilson (fair game) and Herman Wouk (not so fair game) as caterers to the mass values.

Mr. Aldridge's contributions as critic are substantial. Some of his discussions of the relationship between technique and subject matter are penetrating. His willingness to be immediate in formal criticism, knowing that some writers he mentions are bound to be obscure before his discussion is in print, is boldly worth while. It is a breakthrough from the critical practice of waiting for time to make one's subject choices safe. Of course critics must continue to evaluate, at sufficient remove, things that have been done. But they have, also, an obligation, for which reviews are not an adequate medium, to maintain a continuing discussion of what *is* being done. In this Aldridge has been a pioneer.

He has said effective things about the devastating glut of books now produced. He is witty, shrewd, at times downright funny on the proliferation of academic cliques which attempt to secure monopolies over the channels of creative literary production as well as over criticism. For these and other services we are in his debt.

Yet I think I have never seen a critic so stimulating on the particular and so dubiously grounded on the general as Mr. Aldridge. When he is appraising the individual writer or analyzing specific books, he is exhilarating with his caustic sharpshooting, whether one is in agreement with him or not in any given case. When he elaborates about that dubious abstraction, the writer, and the contexts and conditions of his work, some of the assumptions upon which his whole critical structure rests need examination and challenge. I would like to develop a few points on the matter of values and of conformity as they arise in the Aldridge books.

First, consider the relationship between writers and readers. Mr. Aldridge says, "Ideally, the writer and the reader should share the same values, so that the material which the writer selects as valuable enough to write about will automatically be valuable to the reader. But this would depend upon the existence of a society based on certain stable moral assumptions, the sort of society to which . . . we obviously do not belong today."

Now we could turn this around, to emphasize its converse suggestion that what the reader considers valuable enough to read about would automatically be valuable to the writer. If we do this we seem to arrive at the very conformity to mass culture values which, rightly or not, he is lamenting in *In Search of Heresy*. Is the value-sharing between writer and reader actually a factor commensurate with the importance Aldridge assigns to it? Is the writer by nature a filament or a reflector? Is such light as he emanates merely reflected back from the professed values of his era, or is he himself a primary illuminator, a source of light to his era? The minor, negligible writer may simply bounce back some of what he has received. The writer of stature is always on a value level that sets him apart to some extent from his readers, offering a sharply defined, individual evaluation of life which will repel and enrage many (often the majority) and will attract others (generally a minority). It is therefore hard to see how Aldridge can complain that lack of values in our era is the source of weakness in our writers.

Moreover, we have already spoken too much about values before stopping to ask, *what* values? In *After the Lost Generation* he is complaining that there are no values. *In Search of Heresy*, with its cry about conformity, is actually a complaint against some of the kinds of values now current, about one type of that common assumption the absence of which, in a different context, he bewails.

He does not sufficiently define the difference, if there is a difference, between the "mass cultural values" he deplores and the "fund of values, attitudes, customs and beliefs" which he elsewhere says the writer must share with his audience. Did the Victorian writers have any advantage over the present ones? Were the common assumptions of that age any more fruitful for the writer than those of ours? Was conformity any less widespread? Did not mediocre writers, mere sentimentalists, pietists, and moralists, conform and cater to Victorian common assumptions?

Did not Dickens, and Shaw, and Wilde, and Butler, and all truly distinguished writers in their several times and ways, set up value structures in conflict with their era?

Everybody has values of some sort; every age has an area of common ones, of some sort. Discussion of values, to be in any way meaningful, must carry with it some identification. The Marxist has values, the Jew has values, the Christian has values, so has the ethical humanist. These four are curiously overlapped, insofar as virtually the entire value structures of the Marxist and of the ethical humanist are derivations of and variations from the Judeo-Christian value structure. One may ask which of these value structures is the more excellent, but cannot charge any of the four as being without values. Then, of course, the sheer, irresponsible hedonist has values, so do the iconoclast and nihilist of diverse types, so does the "organization man" or the almost faceless dweller in "the lonely crowd."

As for the common values held in any age—that "society based on certain stable moral assumptions," of which Aldridge speaks —we must remember that all mass-based assumptions tend to deteriorate into lip-service and a nullifying taken-for-grantedness. This has always been so, and presumably always will be so. The active life of a value structure is never to be truly judged or appraised except as manifested in individuals, and while there remain individuals vitally attached to and operating within a value structure, it cannot be said to be dead or vanished. At periods when the perennial tides of conformity happen to run particularly high, it is the individuals who profess values, and who attack the false in the name of the real, who are the true heretics, socially speaking, that Aldridge is looking for.

He is often contradictory. After his plea for common assumptions between writer and readers, presumably within a whole society, he asserts in *In Search of Heresy* that only a coterie can afford "protection and support" to the developing writer, who should shun the mass audience. But such coteries, to be acceptable to Aldridge, apparently can only be of the arty "little magazine" variety. If, let us say, a frankly Christian writer such as the extraordinary Charles Williams speaks with special directness to a Christian audience (in addition to other readers), this does not seem to come within Aldridge's terms—it is a coterie of another color.

Our present society is based as much on "certain stable moral assumptions" as any that I know, notwithstanding its conflict of ideologies. The non-Communist West, and especially the English-speaking countries, profess, as societies, the Judeo-Christian value structure. They violate this structure neither more nor less than all societies inevitably violate what they profess as social units. The variations of individual assent or dissent are at one of their periodic high ebbs, but not higher than can be demonstrated in other historical eras of drastic transition and conflict.

The writer's problem today is not the impersonal one of absence of values, but is the everlasting private one of acceptance or rejection, of the *choice* of values. It is profoundly true that the mid-twentieth-century world is one in which these private questions of choice and of acceptance or rejection are extremely hard to make. But they can be made, and are being made, and an era in which they are so hardly made is not an era, as Aldridge would have it, in which the writer has a dearth of material and resources, but an era in which the material and resources are exceptionally rich for those who will use them. The writers (and it is only some of them) who deny and nullify values do so from choice. They are free to do so. But it is not true, as implied by Aldridge, that they can do nothing else, or that their time denies them the resources to do anything else.

Aldridge tends to weight his argument by selecting for examination writers conspicuously impoverished in values, assigning to them an arbitrary importance and significance, while dismissing as unworthy of his attention writers who do not fit his thesis. Those who profess values he brushes off as conformists. Much of his thesis about writers therefore requires strict acceptance of his own premises and his own narrow limitation of the field of discussion.

Aeschylus and Sophocles were conservatives in the Greek value structure. They did not set forth their values as reflectors of the attitudes of the people of their time, though those values had formed the Greek culture and ethos. They set them forth as individual spokesmen precisely because, in their time, these values had declined severely into lip-service and hypocrisy, tending toward the subsequent collapse of their culture. That same threat, I agree, hovers over us as it does in all the periodic crises of culture.

When a society's values are threatened by anything, from outright rejection to lip-service, or the shallow conformity, respectability, and sentimentality that are the outward enactments of lip-service, the individual writer has the choice of helping to hack away at the value structure because he thinks it is crumbling, like Bazarov in *Fathers and Sons*, or of reaffirming it in his own terms by a personal choice of values. The writer, like every other individual, always has this freedom, this option, this difficult and painful responsibility.

Thus it is that Aldridge, though sharp in probing into the specific choices and value espousals that various writers have in fact made, is wrong to assert that our writers today lack moral resources which previous writers had at their disposal, and to assert that the ideological divisions of our own time "have dangerously narrowed the area of subject matter available to writers and, consequently, crippled their means of discovering themselves and their age." Today's arena offers one of the most massive opportunities for dramatic conflict to one who is willing to meet it. If the writer chooses to flee from this arena into a private clinical world of individual sickness, he is free to do so, but must accept the critical evaluation that follows on his choice. Let no one say that all other roads were closed to him by the conditions of his time.

I am amazed at how repeatedly, in a variety of contexts, Aldridge defines the writer as the creature of external cultural-environmental circumstance rather than as a creative prime mover in his own right. It is an attitude which nullifies his summons to heresy. The extent to which any writer's situation is as Aldridge claims them all to be is not evidence of some general condition of writers *in abstracto*. It is simply the index to the failure, limitation, triviality, or mediocrity of the individual writer. We have more occasion and more right to judge the writer for offering us a value-less vision of the world than to judge the world for producing a valueless writer.

What some writers have lost is not an external framework of values, not just this or that set of value concepts. They have lost the basic vision of the nature of their own kind. They not only do not know *who* they are, which is problem enough; they also do not know *what* they are—and that is the ultimate tragedy: for man not to know the nature of man. Indeed, if he knows not what he is, is he any longer man, until he has re-learned himself?

Yet the constant threat of this loss of the full realization of manhood, the periodic susceptibility to it, is one of the basic sufferings of man. Bunyan recognized it in that primitively simple but deeply penetrating account of the Pilgrim's progress. A writer is not to be blamed, out of hand, for reflecting this experience of lostness, indeed it is one of his primary rights and functions. Many authors have assumed great stature as voices of this experience. Dante portrayed it for all ages, but pursued it from the gloomy wood through

Hell to triumph. Kafka is one of the most notable projectors of lostness in this century, and his very lostness itself takes its terms of definition from his Judaic roots. And it is this quality that lends the high tragic element to the richly humane but tormented and erratic novels of Wolfe. He sounded it immediately in the famous prefatory invocation of *Look Homeward, Angel:*

> O waste of loss, in the hot mazes, lost, among bright stars on this most weary unbright cinder, lost! Remembering speechlessly we seek the great forgotten language, the lost lane-end into heaven, a stone, a leaf, an unfound door. Where? When?

Yet some of our writers have not simply forgotten that we are true, unique individuals, but even deny it with almost a kind of glee in the condition. Some, instead of being victims of the loss of the vision of uniqueness of species and uniqueness of the self, have become foremost and aggressive propagandists of the idea that we are not true individuals and free, responsible creatures of God.

There are, of course, some works in which the full vision of man is tacit, or latent, remaining unevoked perhaps due to the scope of the work. This is not so much my concern—although the larger the vision of man the larger the work—as is the work in which the full vision of man is specifically or tacitly denied. But I would like to pursue the effect that a widening vision produces on a work, and to refer, in doing so, to the previously stated fact that everyone has values, at some level or another.

In his contention that great subject matter, along with values, has been inaccessible to the contemporary younger writers, Mr. Aldridge offers, as the peculiar areas still left for them, the subjects of homosexuality and racial conflict. Again I digress to remark that any and all secondary subjects still are aspects of man, and man is the great subject. But to take Aldridge on his own terms, let us consider the subject of racial conflict, his "substitute" for a great subject. Four well-known works serve as interesting examples of the steadily expanding and deepening nature of the subject of racial conflict proportionate to the expanding and deepening vision underlying it. It can in itself, like all else, be projected as narrowly specialized or as universal to man.

In the 1920s, Eugene O'Neill wrote *All God's Chillun Got Wings*. This, well in advance of the time when the race question became a major *cause célèbre*, treated the question of mixed marriage, and the social defiance it involved, as a purely private problem. The value scale which O'Neill employed in this play was that of the right of private personal choice and privilege against a hostile society.

In the 1930s, Richard Wright made a large splash with *Native Son*, indeed a powerful novel. Its value scale, however, was confined to bitter personal indignation and protest against palpable social injustice as being the conditioning factors of a crime. This was fine as far as it went. Enthusiastic critics made comparisons to *Crime and Punishment*, but the really vital difference between the works lies in the range of their value scales.

Not long afterward came Lillian Smith's *Strange Fruit*, again a work of substantial merit and force. Protest against social injustice, less personally motivated than Wright's, was its basic concern, and its value scale was recognizably that of the American political liberal of that decade.

But the post-war 1940s, when by Aldridge's law the diminution of value scales should have been most pronounced, brought the most remarkable of all, Alan Paton's *Cry, the Beloved Country*. It contained within it all the value levels of the other books mentioned but also a great deal more. It specifically affirmed the full vision of the nature of man, in its range from degradation to transcendence, so that while it remains a classic of racial conflict it is also a universal drama of the human condition in a sense and measure not true of any of the other works.

The example of the relation of frame of reference to specific subject matter shows the error of Aldridge's classification of racial conflict as something the writer could turn to *in lieu of* more authentic materials. The very turning to the subject, at any level, is in itself an act of relative valuation. In these four examples we have seen how the work expanded in scope, stature, and implications to fill out the size of the value frame.

Melville, in a preface to an edition of *Moby Dick*, remarked, "There is great virtue in a large and liberal theme, we expand to its bulk. To write a mighty book you must have a mighty theme." Quite true. Notwithstanding minority voices to the contrary, mighty themes lie accessible to the writer's hand today, and with them, for choosing or rejecting, the total, cumulative value resources of the whole history of man. They are neither exhausted nor destroyed. The fruits of psychiatric insight and physical science have not subverted, as Aldridge thinks, but enriched the value heritage, contrary to the testimony of a handful of writers and critics who have not understood either the heritage or the true impact of these sciences.

It is important to see that John Aldridge is not just talking about certain writers who think they live in an age in which values have disappeared. He concurs. It is one of his major theses as critic that the values have disappeared. Inevitably, therefore, he appraises the writer as hamstrung by this circumstance and does not hold him as critically measurable by values. And he necessarily finds special, downright patronizing, categories to contain those writers who do affirm values. He sees them as withdrawn into what he calls outmoded religious orthodoxies, or academic institutional orthodoxies, or slavish conformity to mass values.

The peculiar contradictions of his theory structure lead to some odd expressions in the relation of *In Search of Heresy* to *After the Lost Generation*. Early in the "Search of Heresy" essays he remarks: "The younger novelists who, three or four years previously, had written their first books in a spirit of confidence that they were entering on a new creative cycle and carrying forward an established creative tradition suddenly found themselves high and dry in a world where all they stood for seemed to have gone into eclipse and where they themselves had become premature anachronisms."

He then identifies some of the writers he has in mind: Jean Stafford, Carson McCullers, John Horne Burns, Norman Mailer, Paul Bowles, and Truman Capote. There is a lot of talent in that mix, but what in the name of Heaven could that peculiarly assorted lot ever have been said to have "stood for" that could have gone into eclipse between Aldridge's two books? The precise limitation of their various talents is that they never stood for anything, which I had thought was part of the burden of Aldridge's first book. As a matter of fact that phrase, "all they stood for," meaningless as it is in this reference, sounds suspiciously like some notion of values from someone whose thesis is that the values have disappeared. It is precisely this muddiness, this careless use of words and phrases, that is symptomatic of Aldridge's weakness as a theorizer about writers in general, though he can criticize individuals so succinctly.

Aldridge shows repeated evidence of holding the absurd concept that belief and acceptance, particularly if religious, are *ipso facto* creative-intellectual inhibitors to any live mind. This was Joyce's fallacy, as argued in Chapter Eight. It is a notion which runs through a great deal of critical and sociological writing today, in some instances where the writers would repudiate the overt assertion but make it tacit in all their assumptions.

The fatuity of the assumption is, of course, that it would sweep out virtually every great mind, artist or philosopher in Western civilization, and it would relegate to the backward bench such contemporary minds and talents, in various fields, as Paul Tillich, Reinhold Niebuhr, C. S. Lewis, Charles Williams, J. R. R. Tolkien, François Mauriac, Jacques Maritain, Alan Paton, Dorothy Sayers, T. S. Eliot, W. H. Auden, and Martin Buber.

There are novelists who are beginning to forge their way up, on the heels of the immediate wave of World-War-II books and the follow-up novels of the men who wrote them, and there are others who are not newcomers at all, who represent the affirmation or recognition of values in both familiar and new voices. This is in widely varying degree and they are not all of a kind. Among them, but in no sense a comprehensive list, are John Hersey, the late Morton Thompson, May Sarton, Gladys Schmitt, Brendan Gill, Robert C. Goldston, Donald Wetzel, Bentz Plagemann, Nancy Wilson Ross, Jefferson Young, Gerald Green, J. F. Powers, Gerald Sykes, Worth Hedden, H. H. Lynde, Charles Bracelen Flood, Gerald Warner Brace, William Michelfelder, William Du Bois, Mary Renault, Henrietta Buckmaster, Robert Raynolds, and Jan de Hartog. Our present literary scene sustained great loss in the premature deaths of Morton Thompson and James Agee, each only forty-five years old, each leaving two fine novels. Thompson's *The Cry and the*

Covenant, and Agee's *A Death in the Family*, probably are their best respectively. Each of these men possessed a rich, humane talent.

These represent the kinds of minds, the kinds of affirmations and commitments, the kinds of intellectual force that it is all too easy to forget about, or not know about or care about, if one dwells as critic-commentator in a world circumscribed by Truman Capote, Norman Mailer, Tennessee Williams, James Jones, et al. If you choose to limit your recognition and discussion of contemporary writing, ideas, and values to this carefully constricted field, you indeed can draw a strange, unreal picture of the status and condition of contemporary writing. Step outdoors, boys, and see who's around.

Mr. Aldridge uses a telling phrase in connection with Eliot, of whom he speaks as "going back to" religious orthodoxy. That is not an objective word choice, it is a thesis. There is no "back to" whatever about commitment to a religious orthodoxy; it is not something that *was there*, it is something that *is here*, as vital as at any time in Western Christendom's history.

The peculiar critical blindness on this score is not confined to Aldridge by any means. There is a tendency to assume that the religious commitment of a writer as seen in his work is yet somehow irrelevant to his work. This is nonsense, inasmuch as a religious commitment is pervasive and is relevant to everything in a man's life or to nothing. There is a whole wing of admirers of Dostoevsky who engage in elaborate discussions of him that overlook his central Christian commitment. You could not discuss the work of Martin Buber, who is as much novelist-poet as philosopher, and overlook his identity as a Jew. Everything relevant to a man's life is relevant to a man's work, and nothing more centrally so than fundamental beliefs about life and reality.

A few seasons ago we saw the interesting phenomenon of a front-page review, in the *New York Times Book Review*, of T. S. Eliot's then complete poems and plays, which managed to attempt a survey of his entire body of work while taking no cognizance of the fact that Eliot is a Christian, making instead a mere passing reference to the church as if in recognition of a minor eccentricity in the man. Such phenomena as this, and such attitudes as the Aldridge "back to" view, are the ultimate in insular complacency. When *The Cocktail Party* was produced and subsequently published in this country, it utterly bewildered a number of critics due to the simple circumstance that it is a Christian play, requiring recognition and awareness of the fact and its implications if the work is to be intelligently received. And all the while, Aldridge writes blandly about a world in which belief is impossible, while the believer continues to write about a world in which, as always and forever, belief is difficult.

This leads us, finally, to Aldridge's worries, just now, about conformity as a smothering blanket enfolding the writer. Of course there is a great deal of conformity now, and the era of verbal glut and the popular arts inevitably contributes to it. So does the vast industry of advertising, and so does the popular pulpit of the Norman Vincent Peale genre. This is not a new phenomenon, every age, indeed every decade, sees its appropriate equivalent. But Aldridge is much less of a contributor to this discussion than such social analysts, in their several ways, as Russell Lynes, William H. Whyte, Jr., and David Riesman.

Now as to the word "heresy," it has become a sinister term in the vocabulary of the modern liberal mind, much as has the word "sin." Aldridge, going back to the Greek root of the word heresy, meaning "choice," makes it sound appealing and sets this over against its familiar connotation of "an opinion or doctrine at variance with the orthodox or accepted." This is all right as far as it goes, but whereas in the age of the Inquisition heresy was a poison word, Aldridge wishes to make of it a golden word, connoting rebel in a romantic sense, a referent to something always and absolutely to be desired. This is much too sweeping a simplification of the historical meaning of the word, particularly when it has been introduced in so shallow a context as merely the refusal to conform to mass-culture mores. Aldridge implies not that heresy is sometimes right, but that orthodoxy is always wrong. He ignores the uglier aspect of heresy which Charles Williams has characterized as "obduracy of the mind . . . intellectual obstinacy," which can be both socially and privately destructive when it is mere blind reaction, or prideful and arrogant separationism. Like so much else, it is a matter of context. Actually the word heresy is rather weighty for mere resistance to, or independence from, our fiberglas, TV, and Miltown culture. You don't need a heretic for this, you simply need a man with a modicum of independent taste, idea, and will.

However, Aldridge wants to search for heresy, so we must accept his choice of terms. He is so obsessed with his quest for heresy that any espousal of an orderly, rational, or systematic view of life, or any adherence to institutions, apparently is to be branded sweepingly as conformity. In such drastic case, where are we to go, what is to become of community, and where is that "fund of values, attitudes, customs, and beliefs" (which he complains the writer no longer possesses) to be either generated or preserved?

Freedom is not absolute. Commitment is not necessarily conformity, nor is a reasonable measure of acceptance or adaptation to mores. Anarchy and lone-wolfism are not freedom, either socially or intellectually. A high disdain for all common pattern is not necessarily independence but may sometimes be snobbery and pride.

Aldridge describes Eliot's church affiliation as a pillar which blocks off much of the view but has the convenience of somehow helping him to see more clearly what is left in his field of vision. This is a smug view. A basis of intelligent, free commitment is a premise for evaluation and choice, in both life and art. Conformity is not such free commitment, it is blind, unquestioning, unevaluated following. It is equally common and virulent in middle-class mores and in bohemianism, and it is characteristic of all narrow party-linism, from Communist to Republican.

Aldridge has attacked Herman Wouk as a loathsome conformist and toadier to mass values chiefly because Wouk writes out of a view of a tolerably orderly and rational world and does not aggressively disdain every commonplace in action and character. *The Caine Mutiny*, which he singles out for particular contumely, is, within its limitations, a much more balanced picture of individual experience and character occurrence within a military context than either *The Naked and the Dead* or *From Here to Eternity*, notwithstanding the intensive flashes of accurate random pictures and scenes in the latter books.

To a large measure, considering the work being done by writers whom Aldridge either denigrates or ignores, and the vigorous sniping going on from caustic commentators on our cultural scene, this anguished outcry for heresy is amazingly disproportionate. Aldridge presents himself as a kind of intellectual rebel without a cause, at least without a cause of a size commensurate with his agitation. Consequently he appears to want heresy for the sheer sake of being heretical. This is vacuum-packed heresy, or instant heresy for all effective occasions—all you do is add a subject. Professional non-conformism, like reverse party-linism, is just as binding as the thing from which it reacts.

Meanwhile, in this time of supposedly vanished values and diminished themes, I assert the great, continuing, immemorial theme of the writer—the exploration of his own nature. The great questions are constantly before him, made more searching than ever by the conditions of the world. What am I? Who am I? Whence have I come? Where am I going? Why? And it remains the individual writer's failure to see or retain the true image of the nature of man—an image that has been vital and constant for centuries and remains so—that isolates and demoralizes him. It is about that image that he is compelled, by act or default, to make decisions, whether writing of man's problems from within, his problems from without, or of both.

I do not feel complacent about the values in which I believe, and I do not live by them any better than the next man, or as well as some. In that respect I am like the farmer who refused the county agent's invitation to attend classes on improved methods, saying, "I ain't farming half as good as I know how, now." I am not living half as well as I know how—and that is not peculiar to myself but is the way of us creatures. No one knows this better than a person who has experienced psychotherapy. We do not live as well as we know how. This was Socrates' overoptimism, that if man knew the good he would do it. We know perhaps a limited good and we do not do even that . . . nevertheless, we know a limited good.

I have a standard by which I measure my performance, which helps from time to time to jog it a little more in line with what it might be. The Sermon on the Mount is the law of the Kingdom of God, not the working law of the kingdom of this world. But it is profoundly germane to the kingdom of this world in the sense which I have expressed. To say that we do not, even cannot, fulfill our values does not deny them; it places us in a realistic relationship to their source and gives us insight into our own nature and state.

5

The writer and the clinic

In the course of our married life, my wife and I have read a good many books out loud, a practice which is productive of a variety of rewards and skills and is certainly one way to absorb a book. When *From Here to Eternity* burst upon the waiting world we found ourselves in the home of a friend who had just read it. I said, "We must read that—perhaps we can do it out loud." Our friend said, "Well—you need to know somebody extremely well to read *From Here to Eternity* out loud."

He was right, in more ways than he had in mind. To read much of our contemporary fiction out loud is not only to be slapped in the face by its scabrous aspects, but to discover its frequent paucity of sound and vocabulary, the inanity of much of its dialogue, the monotony of its invective, and the repetitiveness of its narrative devices. The "out-loud test," almost disappearing from usage, is one of the sharpest and soundest measures of the writer's achievement at many levels.

There is a strange enormity involved in the license now freely used by writers in subject matter, situation, and language. Herman Wouk touched on a small phase of it in a passage in his *Aurora Dawn*, a novel which has grown in my esteem as time has passed.

> (The reader is reminded that all quotations of Mr. Marquis's conversations are inaccurate insofar as they have been pruned of certain interjections which ladies and children could not possibly understand. Color and emphasis are lessened thereby. On the other hand, this volume may be safely left in parlors frequented by youngsters who have learned to read but not to discriminate—a commendation not lightly made for all modern novels.)

There is an ironic sidelight on the literary situation. Because the legal regulations and standards of customary practice, which govern newspapers and periodicals, are more restrictive than those relating to books, there are frequent cases where it would be impossible, in newspaper reviews or periodical criticism, to quote fully and extensively from passages under debate. The critic may find himself prevented from exhibiting the thing against which he protests (or which he defends). In the same way, common restraints of taste and a due regard for public opinion (without any question of Nice-Nellyism) limit and inhibit such textual quotation and discussion on the platform or for any public gathering unless in the relatively clinical tone of some classrooms. This is a problem I have run up against in lecturing. We have a literature today a considerable portion of which could not be read aloud in public without inviting either the police or the lynch rope.

Literature is the living voice of man in every age. What men say on the streets, at table, and in rooms, and in the intimacy of their beds, the records of the courts, the clinical data of the physician and analyst, the visions and dreams men have of horror or bliss, of heaven or hell, arc adjuncts to literature. They contribute vitally to literature but are not in themselves literature. They contribute insofar as they provide data and raw materials to help illuminate the interpretation of human events and behavior. But it is not the material, it is that illumination and interpretation of human activity and condition that constitute the true art of fiction.

One of the factors contributing to the odd embarrassments mentioned above is the upsurge of the narrowly clinical in material and treatment. Ira Wolfert has spoken of the danger of the writer "becoming medical and, thus, trivial." The problem of the case-history approach to character is involved here. The psychiatrist knows that his clinical case record is not complete, even though it may be sufficient for therapeutic use. We can never know *all* the facts—it is one of the limitations of being human.

The novelist never knows all the facts. Even Joyce's monumental experiments could not be held to have captured all the data of Leopold Bloom's day or H. C.

Earwicker's night. We understand this limitation, tacitly. But the mediocre writer, trying to tie up and explain his character as if in a clinical case record, produces a false effect of omniscience arising out of the pretense of a hyper-realism or naturalism—common and sometimes convenient words but nevertheless deplorable since reality and nature are not *in* art, although art may be *about* them.

More and more we see in novels and short stories material treated in fashions appropriate only to such clinical case studies as those of, say, Dr. Wilhelm Stekel. I hold, in principle, the belief that no area of human behavior is automatically taboo or precluded from the use of the artist. But the artist is artist—not clinician. The methods and devices of recording and presentation used in the clinic are not appropriate or legitimate for the artist and cannot be employed by him under the pretense that they are art. Novelized, such material is neither true clinical data nor art, but becomes something different from either and not pleasant to contemplate.

Tennessee Williams, in his novel, *The Roman Spring of Mrs. Stone*, and in some of his short stories (perhaps less so in his plays simply because of the police), leads us through the quagmires not merely of homosexuality, but of masochism, sadism, and cannibalism.

A fine example of Mr. Williams at work is in his volume *One Arm, and Other Stories*. Anything in the collection might serve, but let us take a moment for "Desire and the Black Masseur," described on the jacket as a "famous excursion into the logic of the macabre."

A little man of thirty, named Burns, in New Orleans, has "an instinct for being included in things that swallowed him up": family, job. "He had no idea what his real desires were." At a Turkish bath, one day, he finds himself being massaged by a giant Negro masseur. The almost savage ferocity of the ministrations awakened new sensations in Burns, "until all at once a knot came loose in his loins and released a warm flow. . . . So by surprise is a man's desire discovered, and once discovered, the only need is surrender, to take what comes and ask no questions about it. . . ."

Burns continues to frequent the masseur, notwithstanding broken ribs, until one time a leg is broken. The manager throws out both masseur and client. It is near the end of Lent, and what ensues is liberally intermingled with symbols of the Passion, a juxtaposition always popular with our decadents.

Burns is carried to the masseur's own room and there the massage continues for a week until Burns dies— ineffably happy. His last whispered words: " 'You know what you have to do now?' . . . The black giant nodded. . . . The giant began to devour the body of Burns. It took him twenty-four hours to eat the splintered bones clean." He then ties up the "bare white bones" in a croker sack, rides to the end of a streetcar line (named Desire?) and drops them into the lake.

I haven't made it up. I haven't exaggerated. You can buy the book and read it, to see.

Apart from anything else, it becomes abundantly clear at once that Mr. Williams has never eaten a body, or even tried to. If he had, he would know that the thing simply isn't practical, let alone in twenty-four hours, raw—and he would know that the mess is something incalculably fearful before you arrive at those bare, splintered white bones in the croker sack. Why, the man must have eaten enough Southern fried chicken to be able to see how ludicrously he has over-simplified the job. I found myself so distracted by these considerations that I never got around to the "logic of the macabre" for which I'm told the story is famous.

Wandering from Lent in New Orleans to the scene of the shabby vagrant urinating under the balcony of Mrs. Stone's villa in Rome, where she throws the key down to him, we have traversed the representative range of Williams-land and can quietly withdraw. But we will find should we wish, or whether we wish them or not, similar edifications in the novels of Alberto Moravia, Norman Mailer, Nelson Algren, Paul Bowles, and a goodly fellowship of others.

From the writers' colony presided over by Mrs. Lowney Handy have come not only James Jones and Tom C. Chamales, but a writer named Gerald Tesch, with a novel most appropriately named *Never the Same Again*. His publishers hailed Mr. Tesch as "a fresh and important new talent" and said that his novel "breathes the spirit of adolescence in all its frustrations and uncertain joys." The book was so nearly a travesty of its own genre that it disappeared into oblivion, but it had an importance, both because of its source of origin and inspiration and as an example of a tendency run amuck.

Never the Same Again is preoccupied, in the order of their importance, with the prolonged homosexual seduction of a thirteen-year-old boy by a mature man in the course of a summer, retrospection about the seducer's youthful incestuous relations with his own mentally unstable sister, and the broken marriage and somewhat casual amours of the boy's mother, with whom his seducer hovers on the verge of an affair. These are the bald facts of the story.

As to Mr. Tesch's talents, he writes well, characterizes with a good bit of precision and force, and confronts us with some unquestionably authentic human behavior. We can believe this case study all too easily. Yet as a piece of fiction I count it one of the most unwholesome and distasteful items in a wide and long professional experience of reading.

As it is set before us, the story of Johnny Parish and Roy Davies is humanly, but not artistically, tragic. It is a matter of social concern and calls for compassion and therapeutic treatment. To paraphrase Arthur Miller, attention must be paid to such people—but by whom, in what context, and by what methods?

Mr. Tesch, rejecting utterly the arts of suggestion and inference, prolongs, with nauseating insistence, dialogues and actions which the reader has fully and sufficiently comprehended, for the purposes of art, when the author had no more than approached them. His many pages of data of a clinical nature, embedded in a novel, lose the asepsis of the clinic and become noisome and festering—possibly even contagion-breeding. What is to the clinic a necessary examination—as it is medically necessary to examine feces—can be in the novel only a morbid preoccupation. The data of the clinic are for the eye and use of the trained, not for the diverse audience of fiction, and they exist for healing use, not for diversion and titillation.

Tesch has not incorporated in his novel any elements to illuminate, interpret, heal, or redeem the mess which he insists upon detailing so specifically. Neither is he professionally competent, clinically. Some such function can be the only basis for the writer's claim to unlimited freedom in the selection and use of materials. Novels such as *Never the Same Again* jeopardize that freedom by employing it without the responsibility which goes with all freedom.

A pertinent contrast is found in the late Robert M. Lindner's *Rebel Without a Cause* (the title of which was purchased for use with a motion picture of real but limited merit, and which had no connection with the book). This is a non-fiction work presenting the clinical case record, with interpretive comments, of a young criminal psychopath. It is done with an equipment and method, for a purpose and audience quite different from those of the general novel.

Presumably Mr. Tesch is concerned for his boy, Johnny, and the seducer, Roy—and so am I. But while he gives us specific accounts of what they have said and done, he leaves us dark on what it all means and

what could or should be done for them. There is no
visible value assessment whatever concerning this situation—there are neither moral appraisals, medical rec-
ommendations, nor social pleas.

This author knows how to be cryptic and how to
work by indirection at the wrong time and place.
He concludes the story with a series of incidents so
vaguely suggested that we scarcely know whether
Johnny is alive or dead. He could well have been
cryptic and vague about the sexual acts and discussions, and specific about their meaning. He insists on
rubbing our noses in what could be understood clearly
by indirection, yet disdains to let us know the thing
without which this work is a vain exercise—how he,
the artist, evaluates it.

Now, as often in such discussions, it may be asked,
"Has not Mr. Tesch given us an experience?" He has,
indeed, but he has done no more. To give the reader
an experience is only a part, not the whole, of the
writer's function. It is giving us evaluated experience
that distinguishes the great or the good writer,
whether the evaluation be spelled out specifically, or
whether it is tacit in the total context of characters,
actions, and conditions that he sets before us to represent his world. (It is always the writer's world that
we enter in art—never the objective world.)

In his short story, "The Delicate Prey," which is
the title piece for a collection, Paul Bowles describes
with a delicate precision how one Arab mutilates another on no especial provocation. As with much other
hideous material in his stories and novels, Mr. Bowles

narrates these actions precisely with a kind of wide-eyed, innocent wonder—and no comment, tacit or otherwise. In offering this delicate dish for our delectation Mr. Bowles offends more than the equally spelled-out sadisms of Mickey Spillane precisely by the measure and proportion in which his talents and endowments exceed those of Spillane. And if no one in the story, and least of all its author, shows a sign of being revolted or disturbed by this interesting pastime, is there not strong inference for the reader that such actions, at least when performed by primitives, have a certain representativeness and acceptability?

Herman Wouk, as quoted at the beginning of this chapter, spoke of those "who have learned to read but not to discriminate." It is not only youngsters of whom this can be true. Our clinical writers have learned to write but not to discriminate. Actual social harm, indeed, may result from this, but we should not have to look so far for a deterrent factor. The clinical approach is artistically indefensible.

For contrast to the common contemporary use of the clinical detail and the unevaluated presentation of such experience, I suggest the three chapters omitted from the original edition of Dostoevsky's *The Possessed*, but published in recent years under the title *Stavrogin's Confession*, translated by Virginia Woolf and S. S. Koteliansky. The subject of the confession, quite harmonious with the current vogue, is the rape of a twelve-year-old girl. The circumstances leading to this action are set forth fully, in mounting emotional-psychological-moral tension, reaching a culmi-

nating sense of horror at the moment of the act itself.
But as to narrative method in presenting this material
—the preparation of the ground is so thorough that
the nature of the act is clear and unmistakable. The
aftermath of the act is similarly developed. The act
itself is not described. Why should it be? It does not
need to be. What purpose could be served? Yet the
schools of the Messrs. Williams, Mailer, Algren, Tesch,
and Bowles, et al., would probe for the limits of the
law in spelling out the action of this rape, while leaving out all that concerns Dostoevsky.

Now undoubtedly Dostoevsky, too, has given us an
experience—an appalling and painful one, but entirely
legitimate for the artist, as is any form of human experience or action. But he has omitted what only the
doctor or the court of law might have legitimate need
to pursue in detail. And he has not dropped this experience into our laps unevaluated, for us to grope for
some meaning in it.

He shows us a man under the burden of guilt. This
disclosure is called a confession, and it is made, both
orally and in writing, to a monk, though not in the
formal context of the confessional box. While it is
shown that human beings are capable of such actions,
and while compassion is displayed for them, there is
no doubt about the obloquy, outrage, and guilt of the
deed. We are told that a man has an immortal soul
which is jeopardized by such acts, but that even these
acts have not precluded either the mortal or immortal
salvage, redemption, and rehabilitation of that soul.
This, then, is a total, not a partial, comment on the

human character and condition—and this is something universal, containing truths for all sorts and conditions of men. There is, then, a productive reason or purpose for Dostoevsky to have afflicted us vicariously with such experience. Neither the materials nor the methods of evaluation of Dostoevsky are required of any writer, but the artistic obligation is the same for all who wish to make any claim to stature.

The humane genius of Dostoevsky is not content to leave this matter simply at the level of confession and absolution. As a matter of fact absolution is refused, or rejected, by the guilty Stavrogin himself, and when Father Tikhon discerns that the crisis of guilt and self-hate is so great in Stavrogin that another crime is imminent, the tormented man cries out, "You cursed psychologist!" and flees from the monastic cell.

Stavrogin, in his written confession, is insistent that "I am always master of myself when I want to be. And so let it be understood that I do not claim irresponsibility for my crimes, either on account of environment or of disease."

But Tikhon, when he has read the self-excoriating document thrust into his hands, says to Stavrogin, "Yes, it is repentance and natural need of repentance that has overcome you. . . . But you, it seems, already hate and despise beforehand all those who will read what is written here, and you challenge them. You were not ashamed of admitting your crime; why are you ashamed of repentance? . . . Certain passages in your statement are emphasized; you seem to be luxuriating in your own psychology and clutch at each detail, in order to surprise the reader by a callousness which is not really in you. What is this but a haughty defiance of the judge by the accused?"

An important aspect of man's condition that is related to this question of the clinical is the demonic—whether one believes in it as literal, or in some sense of symbol and fantasy. Often in Dostoevsky we are dealing with the demonic, and we encounter it vividly in Jacob Wassermann's *The World's Illusion*. I have seldom seen it more intensely evoked than in Ben Hecht's superb long short story, *Death of Eleazer*.

Shirley Jackson, John Cheever, and John Collier all have employed the demonic in their work, brilliantly though often relatively shallowly, as if for the sheer relish of novelty or fantasy. Incidentally, as a clinical character study well assimilated into art, not necessarily involving the demonic, Miss Jackson's *The Bird's Nest* is a unique and fascinating achievement that makes most interesting parallel reading with the later non-fiction, clinical case study, *The Three Faces of Eve*, by Doctors Thigpen and Cleckley.

The truest, deepest senses of the demonic are captured by the novels of J. R. R. Tolkien, C. S. Lewis, and Charles Williams. They all have the kind of greatness that is expressed well by T. S. Eliot, in respect to Williams, in that "there is nothing else that is like them or could take their place."

Why are so many writers currently preoccupied with clinical behavior patterns, from the simply neurotic to the psychopathic? Is it because, as we read, mental illness is on the rise? Commenting in terms of the familiar figures in newspapers that incidence of cancer is two-to-ten, of heart disease, three-to-ten, and the like, a reputable psychiatrist has said the incidence of mental illness is one-to-one, at some time or another, in some degree or another. We are all subject to the common cold and to mental-emotional disorders, though we do not all suffer pneumonia or paranoia.

There is a valid question as to whether mental illness is on the rise as much as intelligent awareness of it is on the rise. We see an abundance of mental illness throughout all literature and history, unremarked as such. Today there are new forms of awareness and understanding which, naturally, involve the writer's work as an interpreter of character and behavior. It is not only proper that it should be so—it would be a judgment upon a writer to be unaware of or unresponsive to new data on human life. But sound knowledge, maturity, and responsibility are necessary when he ventures into specific use of clinical problems or materials.

Some writers visibly are compulsive in their use of clinical materials—their books are symptoms more than creations. They are more than preoccupied with the sick, they are unable to see the well. Some use such materials with calculated cynicism, for their shock and sensation value. Some, between these extremes, are guilty of no more than a muddled and mediocre use of clinical materials neither more nor less conspicuous than the muddled and mediocre use they make of the other materials of life.

The mess that the writer may make with his clinical materials, and the distortion in which he projects their relationship to life, often is directly related to the distortion or loss of his vision of man. This can be a sorrowful thing to see. Truly to understand a man who is sick you must understand a man who is well. I believe that the loss of the understanding of the full nature of man is itself a major source of sickness. Yet I do not suggest that the true knowledge of man is an easy healing of ills, or a happy and blithesome thing. Sometimes it can be a somber and terrifying thing to contemplate man's full measure of freedom and responsibility, and both his nearness to and alienation from his Creator God.

The mark of the true artist is to know what needs to be told and what needs to be said, and to tell and say neither more nor less within the context of the actions with which he is concerned. Who is to judge in this matter? The artist must judge in the first instance, and the critic has the right and duty to express opinion on the artist's judgment.

The publisher should judge, in terms of the standards he sets in appraising the worth or value of material considered for publication. The principle that the publisher must be free to publish what he thinks is truly of worth does not mean that he simply publishes anything without responsibility for its standards of value. Publishers have a responsibility, which cannot be evaded, for some of the grossest excesses of our writers, particularly in terms of the descriptions offered, and the claims made, for books in some cases, and in more flagrant instances, for the frank promotional exploitation of sensationalism. Publishing should never be pimping. There is more than a laugh to the *New Yorker* cartoon showing a publisher happily talking to an author and saying, in effect, "Your action moves swiftly, your characters are well developed, and what's more, you have a very dirty mind."

The book-buying public also has a responsibility, for there are those who will purchase anything that promises a new titillation, even when they are totally indifferent to the artistic context in which it may occur, or quite incapable of judging whether there is an artistic context or not.

I would resist vigorously the censorship of any of the books I have singled out for attack. At the same time, I call for a more clear line of distinction between material in the form and uses of literary art, and material that is little more than a crude and faulty approximation of the playback of a clinical interview.

6

The death of Mrs. Grundy

Nowadays, almost every writer, good or bad, when he begins to write about sex, lapses into a ritual of clichés. The reader sees it coming and generally can tell, after a line or so, which of the several standard gambits he is about to get this time.

How stale, flat, and unprofitable they all are! Many writers are deluded into thinking that a four-letter-word vocabulary, carefully detailed scenes of undressing, and clinically direct anatomical descriptions add up to a profound study of the relations between men and women. This is quite as fantastic a belief as would be the notion that the corn of soap operas represents tragedy. The disaster lies in the fact that a good many of our writers, readers, and critics seem unaware of the quality of sexual-soap-opera which permeates even the more serious modern writing. Some of our most respected literary figures, such as Edmund Wilson, have been among the worst blunderers.

The criteria for every detail about sex in fiction

should be: What does this illumine? What does it reveal that was not known before or that cannot be left as tacitly understood? Does this add anything to our understanding of character that was not already clear? In most cases, the matter offered us, as if conforming to an unwritten code of ritualistic minimum requirements, has now become so wearisomely shopworn that it serves none of the above useful purposes or much of any other ones.

Today we have specialists in various aspects of sex, as well as those who cull a little from each. There are undressing specialists who give us an accounting of every several button, strap, and bow, layer by layer, garment by garment. James M. Cain established the now large school of clothes-ripping technicians, who have shredded enough lingerie to clothe the poor of the world. It does, I suppose, tell us something about Mr. Cain's characters when they rip off each other's clothing, as they nearly always do. It also tells us a good bit about Mr. Cain and his confreres in this particular craft. James Jones contributed shorts-shucking, which follows halter-dropping in sequence. In their quaint naïveté, some of the older writers, at a certain point, relied on the reader to realize that somewhere along the line some clothing very likely came off—how much, in what order, and by whom removed somehow doesn't seem to have mattered. Tolstoy refrained from bothering us over any problems Vronsky may have had with Anna's underwear.

There are specialists in the texture and surface temperature of the body, ranging in the first case from marble to velvet; in the second, from hot to cool, which is partly seasonal; in summer fiction they tend to be cool. There are also body-geography and sexual-topology students—erotic spelunkers of a sort. The promising phrase "dark recesses" is current in an amazingly resourceful range of reference.

There are specialists in biting and punching: (a) in acquiescence, (b) in resistance. This is related to the popular scene of rape, with or without preliminary physical disablement. Army medics know a category called the walking wounded. Mickey Spillane has created a category of the osculatory, or kissing wounded, in his sex-with-a-boot-or-a-bullet-in-the-belly school. One rewarding night I heard Edward R. Murrow ask Mickey Spillane why he writes the kind of books he does, getting the luminous answer: "I write the kind of books I want to read and can't find." This is a farther-reaching motivation for writers at all levels than is imagined.

We have experts in the functional mechanics and general physics of sex relationships. Many writers seem compelled to diagram precisely what is involved in sexual intercourse, either to let the reader know, or to reassure themselves that they haven't forgotten. Some of their novels could be moved from the fiction section to the "Do It Yourself" shelf. The insistence on penetration by some of them has overtones as revealing as those of the Latin tradition of showing the stained sheets after the bridal night.

Other writers make a fetish of form and shape, in the general and in the particular. Buttock and bosom are the major concentrations in this field, but we shouldn't forget the popular "those mighty thighs" division. We find connoisseurs in the fine art of fruit analogy, involving pears, melons, peaches, apples, and grapes. The grain cereals have fallen into disuse, which is a pity, for the author of the Song of Songs did well with a heap of wheat.

There has arisen a formidably complex school of orgasm symbolism. Hervey Allen was one of its early pioneers, with the concentric ripple. Water offers so many possibilities that we also find waves, high tide, general sensations of sinking and drowning, also floating, and occasionally whirlpools. The immemorial scene of the nude moonlight swim, in salt or fresh water, holds its place firmly among our non-fertility rites. Warm, dry sand, or pine needles, used to be satisfactory couches for the inevitable consummation. Lately, however, since the modified screenplay distantly related to *From Here to Eternity*, fornication in the surf has become the desideratum, so that the brief tussle in the sea foam has now become a standard image of suggestion, and when the waves keep on breaking in, all by themselves, you know what's happening.

Among the orgasm symbols are the high-wind group, the fire group, and the rocket or levitation group. Fireworks are popular and have been deemed sufficiently refined even for Grace Kelly films. Earthmoving was the unique contribution of Ernest Hemingway. There has been nothing to match it before or since.

The cult of brutality runs the full gamut of sadism and masochism. Its unsavory variations generally are little more than ingenious elaborations of the classical bite, preferably with ensuing salty taste which may be tears or blood, but blood is better.

Lastly, best left without too much discussion, there are the accompanying-sound-effects school, the "I-shouldn't-have-kept-on-watching-but-I-did" gambit, and the part that begins, "Tell me about the others." Nancy Hale, Ben Hecht, Frederic Wakeman, and James Jones have done especially big things with the last.

Now, in the language of jacket blurbs, how "bold, frank, fearless, honest, realistic, and profound" can you get? I haven't made up any of these exhibits, but have read them over and over, in the line of professional duty. Except for those peripheral phenomena which even now are rapidly being used up, just about every possibility you can think of in sex has been boldly, frankly, and interminably explored. The law of diminishing returns—which an amiable woman once asked President Wilson to repeal—has done its deadly work.

Today, exhausted writers are searching frantically for novelty where no novelty is possible. This has at least something to do with the increasing prevalence of fringe-type and abnormal relationships in novels. No other punch, no other shock, is left.

In consequence, those standard classics of border-line pornography, politely known as "erotica," have become pale, wan, and obsolete beside the common modern novel. Sacher-Masoch and De Sade crumble pitiably before Cain and Spillane, Mailer and Jones, Algren and Tennessee Williams, Paul Bowles and Edmund Wilson. Louys, Petronius, and Ovid are quite o'ertopped. "The Feast of Trimalchio" is a woman's club luncheon beside some of the parties in current fiction. Even aging Henry Miller has found it impossible to remain beyond the pale. The strain has told on him. He has given up and abandoned sex for travelogues on a larger scale. A man cannot get himself privately published any more.

Alas! Mrs. Grundy is dead. Her passing, surprisingly, ushered in an evil day. She had been sitting for a long time on the lid of a kind of Pandora's box, the opening of which had come to represent the *summum bonum* to a generation of writers. Lo, now, the box has been open these many years and the scourge is upon us!

A long, hard fight was fought for the right of the serious literary artist to deal as he sees fit with any facet of human behavior, with no arbitrary taboos on language, and no forbidden areas in the relationships between the sexes.

This fight was fought for serious purposes by the honest artist. The privilege so hard won is merited only by him, and the check-rein against its abuse lies in the stature and responsibility of the artist himself. It is not a privilege to be lavished on every idiot or pornography merchant. None—absolutely none—of society's other important privileges in areas involving

discretion and judgment—even the driving of an automobile—is lavished simply on anyone. There is no
reason why this privilege of literary license should be.
Yet it is—and I admit that nothing directly restrictive
can be done about it without opening the doors to the
censor again. But unless something is done we are inviting the censor by provocation, so that plain-speak-
ing about the matter within the book trade is in order,
and overdue. Editors and critics, publishers and book-
sellers, have a discriminatory responsibility here as
large as that of the writers.

The terrible mistake made by some writers, once
their freedom had been established, was the failure to
realize that it was not a freedom required for everyday
use by every Tom, Dick, and Harry writing his little
story. They took the green light as a dare and have
made what should be a last resource serve as a stock-
in-trade. Full freedom of subject and language is now
a part of the writer's working equipment. But every
craftsman has tools used rarely, for the special problems or extraordinary circumstances. He does not em-
ploy them except when the other tools won't do—and
they keep their edges, accordingly, so that when used
they are effective.

If any major insights into character have been
achieved in modern fiction, going beyond the work
of earlier men, they have not been achieved by piling
up sexual details. To choose what might seem to be a
least-promising example from an older school, Charles
Dickens, for all the Victorian constraint and claptrap,

achieved in *Dombey and Son* a powerful depiction of a horrible marriage in which all its sexual realities can be read by the discerning.

The error of confusing cumulative detail with interpretive insight explains the paradox that so many of our most lurid and violent writers today have no comprehension whatever of passion. When Mark Twain's wife tried to shock him out of swearing by reciting a string of oaths he laughed at her and said, "You know the words, my dear, but you don't know the tune."

The tune and measure of true passion are missing from the unrestrained words in most current writing about sex. Take a look, for contrast, at Chapter Eleven of Part Two of *Anna Karenina*, in which Tolstoy shows us the impact, emotionally, upon Anna and Vronsky, of the first consummation of their love. Or read the passages of ungovernable passion between Jean-Christophe and Anna Braun, the wife of his friend, as Romain Rolland delineates them. Where have these insights into the sexual experience of the human creature been surpassed? What could be added to them by the four-letter-word or anatomical-chart approach? Such expedients could only diminish the effect.

Part of the present fallacy was and is a by-product of the impact of Freud. But as there were brave men living before Agamemnon, there were profound analysts of behavior working in literature before Freud. Ill-digested, unassimilated, partially grasped Freudianism (as contrasted to a true assimilation of the insights to which Freud contributed so tremendously) has led some writers to attempt a crude, simulated case-history method in drawing their characters.

Will they not understand that once the author has brought the relationship between a man and a woman to a certain stage, there is seldom need for the author or reader to know more? It may often be the clinical problem of the psychoanalyst to know more. But perhaps the author or reader who thinks he must witness the last details of an established intimacy is also the problem of the psychoanalyst.

It seems inconceivable, reading *Sister Carrie* today, that it ever was a *cause célèbre*. It is chaste as new snow in language and detail. Dreiser's battle, always the important battle, was over the right to portray honestly the social realities of sex relationships. In part, Farrell fought this battle, too, but he fell prey to the great fallacy. His work, unlike Dreiser's, has suffered from wearisome repetition and self-defeating misuse of what is commonly called obscene speech, in the name of that basic freedom he demands rightly.

Joyce is a particularly revealing case. In *Dubliners* and *A Portrait of the Artist as a Young Man* he worked essentially within the bounds of conventional restraint. *Ulysses* is something else again. It is a major work, whether its value is to be considered mainly historical or intrinsic. It is a landmark in literary history, and in its magnitude as a creative experiment in form and conception is a perfect example of the instance in which the artist earns and deserves defense against any constraint or censorship. But I think it is not too harsh to say each writer's work must show cause, as does *Ulysses*, not in the eyes of the Comstocks and the cops, but in the eyes of his literary contemporaries, in terms of its degree of contribution, why it should be granted the maximum of freedom.

I throw out a challenge to novelists. When you write your scenes involving sex, see what you can do with the resources that have sufficed for the greatest literature thus far produced. When you have done work of such power and scope within these limits that it is obvious your concepts require the ultimate batteries—go ahead. The rest of the literary fraternity will have to back you up if you should get in dutch. But do we have to fight for the artistic integrity and creative freedom of Mickey Spillane, or for dozens of other more pretentious, but cheap and trashy, imitators of better men? Can not some of that problem be solved at our editorial desks, and some more of it met in our pages of criticism and review?

For heaven's sake, let us treat our hard-won, vital privilege as a privilege and a responsibility. Don't toss in all the resources out of downright laziness, or lack of talent, or self-indulgence. If a man cannot play, he will produce no better sound on a Stradivarius than on a common fiddle. The mediocre writer takes the highest privilege of his art and debases it, abuses it, exploits it, and forces his fellows to defend against censorship what is often artistically indefensible. Many a talented writer dulls his gift by substituting cheap and easy sensationalism for costly and difficult exploration of human passion.

Today's writer works practically without limits. Yet, as Goethe said, "It is in working within limits that the craftsman reveals himself." The limits imposed by the late Mrs. Grundy's rule forced the craftsman to do his job the hard way. When she was deceased the era of attempted short cuts began, and like many other attempted short cuts in modern society it was a snare and a delusion.

Restraint must be applied by writers and editors and publishers themselves, or we will pile up so much ammunition in the hands of the censorious that they will make our vulnerability in the field of taste and self-restraint an entering wedge for censorship in everything, including ideas. Mrs. Grundy is dead. Let us not give the old lady a new lease on life!

7

The female zombies

Rich, complex portraits of women are not common in recent fiction or, indeed, in the fiction of any period. Brilliant as they are, consider how particular and how circumscribed in range are such *tours de force* as Thackeray's Becky Sharp and Flaubert's Emma Bovary. It is odd that the most striking successes in realizing and evoking the feminine nature, relative to time and social context, belong to that bearish and tempestuous man, Leo Tolstoy, in his splendid creations of Natasha Rostov and Anna Karenina.

Tolstoy's contemporary and compatriot, Dostoevsky, although his peer as novelist and belonging in the small, select group of acknowledged "greats," was no more successful than many lesser men as a characterizer of women. The women of his pages, from Grushenka to Katerina Ivanovna, are interesting and believable in their way, but are not rounded out as beings.

Nicholas Berdyaev has said: "Woman never appears as an independent being for . . . Dostoevsky was interested in her solely as a milestone on the road of man's destiny. His anthropology is masculine: the soul is primarily the masculine principle in mankind and the feminine principle is the inward theme of man's tragedy, his temptation." Of his principal female characters, there is "not a great woman among them, not a single female type with any value of her own. It is always man who is tortured by a tragic destiny, of which woman is only the interior expression."

The difficulties in the characterization of women, by male or female writers, in all literature arise essentially out of the secondary or inferior position which she has occupied in some phases of history, and out of the ambiguous and uncertain position which has been, and is still, hers in supposedly more enlightened eras. Woman, in short, is a being whose status and nature have been uncertain in the eyes of the artist precisely because they have been uncertain in society and in woman's own heart and mind. This is why the woman writer has not necessarily been more successful than the male—either she has projected an image accepted from a male world, or she has expressed some partial aspect or other of the unresolved search of her own sex for individual identity.

Distorted images of woman, and confusions about her sexual bond with men, are particularly conspicuous in current literature, especially in the works of a few representative and highly regarded male writers in whose novels women are seen wholly as sexual objects projected from male attitudes. These portrayals carry large implications about sexuality in general and the nature of women in particular. We will have a long look at some of these portraits and then pursue a tentative effort to evaluate and account for such images. We will try, too, to suggest a view of the sexuality of man which is at least reasonably in harmony with the general tradition of the nature of man which is central to this book.

In the novels of the "after the lost generation" group of writers, whose work has preoccupied John Aldridge and others of the younger people both reading and writing today, we see women frequently from the perspectives of homosexual writers as well as of homosexual characters within the stories. We get, from these, a few remarkably "sensitive" vignettes of wraithlike and lost older women, or of quivering girls trembling at the threshold of adolescence to whom some drastic traumatic experience happens—nine times out of ten stumbling upon a couple in the sex act. There is somewhat of a plethora of sensitivity nowadays, incidentally; far from being a rarity, as a friend of mine observed, "they sell it off pushcarts."

The writers of the harder school are not necessarily more masculine, just more worried about it. Of these, the prophets and pacemakers are James Jones and Norman Mailer, who dominate or inspire a large contingent. In their books, women are not people but are objects. They have no human identity or individuality, no true personality or authentic psychology. They are projections of male attitudes, assumptions, and visions, tricked out with spurious shells of personality and artificially determined (and deterministic) psychologies of the oversimplified case-history type.

The two well-known ladies in *From Here to Eternity* are excellent cases in point. For sheer unreality, the celebrated Lorene, a senior staff worker in Mrs. Kipfer's Hawaiian cathouse, takes some kind of cake. Even her name is given a value: "There was a name for you. Lorene. That was no whore's name, that was a really truly woman's name, Lorene." Some pages later, in a quick reversal, it has become "such a perfect whore's name. . . . It had all the right sounds, the right connotations." Anyway, it turns out to be merely a *nom de bedroom*, for her real name is Alma. Prewitt wants to marry her. "Didn't all the old timers like Pete Karelsen always say whores made the best wives? Whores knew how to appreciate the little things, didn't they say, after they've been down and out."

But Lorene doesn't even seem to be down and out. She appears to be well placed by aptitude, and to have a true vocation. She works frightfully hard and keeps long hours. Prewitt sometimes has to stand in line most of the night to get a turn, at the store. But when Lorene gets her week end off, what does she do but go right home to shack up with Prewitt. This is true dedication, and includes shelling out money, at times, as in the classical whore-pimp relationship.

Various images we are given of Alma-Lorene are quite striking. There is the time that she and her friend Georgette are nursing Prew through illness on his prolonged AWOL, when, on the faces of the two big-hearted whores there "was the same beaming lambency like on some painter's *St Anne and Madonna cuddling St John and Jesus.*"

On the deck of the *Lurline*, as the Jones epic has progressed from here to at least a good, long, wearisome stage toward eternity, Karen Holmes encounters the bereaved Alma-Lorene. "She wondered . . . from her poise and carriage, if the girl was not perhaps a movie star caught over here on vacation by the blitz and unable to get home any sooner. . . . She looked remarkably like Hedy Lamarr. . . . She turned and smiled at Karen slowly out of the lovely childlike face. . . . She has a face like a Madonna, Karen thought exquisitely. Watching her was like being in an art gallery."

Here we should break into these samples of the great American whore mystique to check the background. Alma-Lorene-Madonna-Lamarr is not an ultra-expensive, by-appointment-only call girl of the class associated with periodic newspaper scandals. She is a brutally hard-working, harassed, three-dollar army whore whose condition can be related to the Jones fantasy only in the realm of the soldier's sex dream.

"One rather hates to leave it," observes this piece of four-in-one femininity, staring back at Diamond Head and speaking, I presume, like Billie Dawn taking her diction lessons in *Born Yesterday*.

The projection of the novel's other heroine, Karen Holmes, is less openly ludicrous, but equally lifeless, and equally the product of a male state of mind. She is a good upper-middle-class girl, married to a lieutenant. "I want to go to bed with you," says Sergeant Warden conversationally, standing unannounced on his very first appearance at her door. The finesse of this approach is immediately rewarding. "All right," says Karen, indifferently. Within a few pages, after they've first been interrupted by the unexpected entrance of her young son, who is quickly shooed away, Karen is crying, "I never knew it could be like this" (a prime cliché of the modern sex scene) and thus a great, poignant and compassionate contemporary love story has got under way.

With Jones' crude attempt at case-history tracing, the characteristics of Karen's behavior are attributed to her grim marriage to Lieutenant Dana Holmes, her hysterectomy as a result of getting the clap from him, and her curious employment of the troglodytic Maylon Stark as what she calls "the instrument I used to clean myself." This muddled and chaotic character delineation is suffused with bouts of sophomoric philosophizing about marriage, or such concepts as "the eternal degradation of being a woman," which Karen savors at certain moments.

When probing scrutiny is directed upon the question of what Jones can do well as a writer the area of accomplishment shrinks away to a small patch. The ability to characterize living, believable women is not within that patch. He offers us female zombies performing lifelessly at the command of his will as storyteller. Yet this is the stuff, together with the muddled and nearly paranoid social perspectives analyzed earlier as "the new compassion," which was singled out to receive the accolade of the National Book Award.

Jones' second novel, *Some Came Running*, which became available too late for extensive discussion in this book, contains the same characteristics in its delineation of women. Gwen French, his major attempt to create a non-sexual, sensitive, educated woman, and whom he has wrought in what he conceives to be the image of Emily Dickinson, remains "made up," never comes to life. In spite of painstaking attempts to develop her convincingly he fails to create a credible psychology for her.

His conception of how sex relations are approached remains much the same as in the earlier book. Reminiscent of Warden's approach to Karen, when Dave Hirsh, at his first meeting with Gwen, is invited to visit her and her father, he "casually" asks, "If I do, will you sleep with me?" The novelty here is that she won't.

The prevailing attitudes of Dave Hirsh, the book's hero, toward women have a familiar tone. Dave resents the amenities of courtship. "Why the hell should I have to cater to some goddamned woman just to make her?"

The true voice of Dave rings in his epic line to Ginnie Moorehead: "I don't like to see you picking your goddamned nose when I'm getting ready to take you home and go to bed with you." Here love among the troglodytes has sprung to full flower.

When he marries Ginnie, Dave remembers "the famous oldsoldier's saying about the fact that 'whores make the best wives, because theyre grateful.' " Thus, for all the drastic transition from army to civilian life, Jones' conception of the fabric of human existence is woven on the same old loom.

The distortions in Norman Mailer's view of life are more subtle and devious. For one thing, there are a better mind and a better basic talent at work. But none of his books projects the image of a living woman, least of all *The Deer Park*, with its primary figures, Elena Esposito and Lulu Meyers, although it is quite possible that a living woman might possess the psychotic configurations of either.

Since he ran out of the subject of war, sex has seemed to Mr. Mailer to be the great uncharted continent for the writer to explore. It is hardly uncharted in our generations, yet for Mailer the possibilities of the senses and of sexuality apparently stand as a limitless and commanding preoccupation. He and the Italian Moravia make pallid the sexuality of *Lady Chatterley's Lover*, for they have pursued their subject into the hinterlands of deviation, anomaly, and perversion, all under a gloss of intellectuality and artiness.

At the end of that shambles, *The Deer Park*, we find ourselves abruptly out of bed and face to face with philosophy.

As the supposed thought of the great director Eitel, we have heard, "One cannot look for a good time, Sergius . . . for pleasure must end as love or cruelty . . . or obligation."

This gives rise to the final meditation of the book's narrator, Sergius O'Shaugnessy:

I would have told him that one must invariably look for a good time since a good time is what gives us the strength to try again. For do we not gamble our way to the heart of the mystery against all the power of good manners, good morals, the fear of germs, and the sense of sin? Not to mention the prisons of pain, the wading pools of pleasure, and the public and professional voices of our sentimental land. If there is a God, and sometimes I believe there is one, I'm sure He says, "Go on, my boy. I don't know that I can help you, but we wouldn't want all *those* people to tell you what to do."

There are hours when I would have the arrogance to reply to the Lord Himself, and so I ask, "Would you agree that sex is where philosophy begins?"

But God, who is the oldest of the philosophers, answers in His weary, cryptic way, "Rather think of Sex as Time, and Time as the connection of new circuits."

Then for a moment in that cold Irish soul of mine, a glimmer of the joy of the flesh came toward me, rare as the eye of the rarest tear of compassion, and we laughed together after all, because to have heard that sex was time and time the connection of new circuits was a part of the poor odd dialogues which give hope to us noble humans for more than one night.

Mr. Mailer's double talk about time and new circuits remains undeveloped, left at the end to its quiet meaninglessness, as befits it. His glimmers of "the joy of the flesh," however, are refracted on every page of the novel from one facet or another. I would object less to this exposition if there were some rational note of discrimination in it. But like the rest of his school, who delight to portray what is palpably false in human relations, he will introduce a ludicrous sentimentality into an impossible context and pass it off for a moment of high love. Thus, as Sergius and Lulu Meyers lie on the bed where he has gasped out his traumatic account of war shocks, Sergius tells us:

> She was good that night. . . . It was the best night we ever had, for I loved her and I think she loved me. We passed into each other, and long afterward lay looking at one another and smiling. "I love you," I kept whispering to her, and her eyes filled with tears. "I feel like a woman for the first time," she said. Yet, before I left, our mood changed again. . . . For each of us knew that there was nowhere to go after this night.

Putting aside the grotesque context of relationships in which this touching moment occurs, I am interested in its concluding thought. Early in the book the same note had been sounded in a drunken woman's lament over a dead love. "If he hadn't died, we'd have killed it. The great thing is when something good hasn't time to be spoiled."

Here we have the strain of counter-romanticism, the reverse image of Cyranoism. The romantics of an earlier era, as in *Cyrano de Bergerac* which is a late-flowering of a much older plant, cherished the idea of unrequited love, precisely because it could remain an idealization, hence unchanged, untouched by the world, free of the necessity of coming to any painful maturity of its own essence, free of the necessity to prove itself.

The counter-romantics of our time requite love at the drop of a halter and they have no ideal image to preserve. They celebrate with purple pulsations casual unions of the flesh, then cry out in their piping tragic squeaks that there's nowhere left for love to go. They can only lament it, or seek to renew it in other encounters of equal brevity and finality.

The fear of venturing upon sustained relationships is a common disorder and is, whatever else may be involved in it, a symptom of immaturity. The fact that it is so much a part of our experience makes it a natural subject for the writer. Maturity in the artist requires him to recognize this fear of sustained relationship, this inability to embark upon it, for the special condition that it is. But many of them, themselves possessed by it, or unable to observe beyond it, present the ephemeral moment of the flesh in a puerile philosophy that affirms or implies that it is the summit reality of the human encounter, the inescapable fact of life and love.

The rise of the great whorehouse mystique is another highly specialized phenomenon. It has nothing to do with compassion for the tragedy of prostitution, which has been reflected in literature for centuries. It is a gleeful sort of thing which implies a true vocation for women by both laughingly and lachrymosely sentimentalizing them at the same time; and if the brothel is seen as woman's true vocation, it is seen, too, as man's true haven. The preoccupation of some writers with this scene and subject is extraordinary. They have forgotten, to borrow Polly Adler's phrase, that "A House Is Not a Home."

We have encountered this in both Jones and Mailer (*The Deer Park* focusing its attention more specifically on call girl and pimp). Steinbeck is an apostle of the big-hearted whore when in his *Cannery Row* vein, and *East of Eden* is dominated by the brothel—in fact, too many brothels spoil the book.

William Faulkner contributed largely to whore-house-and-madam lore in *Sanctuary*. That, however, has become such a particular and interesting study, since he has appended *Requiem for a Nun* to further elucidate the life of Temple Drake, that it is too large and complex to pursue here. With his sequel, Faulkner did unmistakably lift *Sanctuary* to a different level and category, whatever the other successes or failures of the venture.

A. B. Guthrie, after having built up his superb picture of the developing West in *The Big Sky* and *The Way West*, falls into the bottomless pit of whorehouses to the nearly total destruction of his third volume, *These Thousand Hills*, which becomes so bedded down in the brothel that the reader begins to wonder what thousand hills are the referent of his title.

The late Madison Cooper's two-volume *Sironia, Texas* was touted, or pimped, as the longest novel ever written, longer than either *War and Peace* or the

Bible. There was really nothing one could say about it, unless to parrot Edmund Waller's famous dictum about *Paradise Lost,* "If its length be not its principal merit it hath no other." Yet for all this mass, paraphrasing Mark Twain, I think if the whorehouse sequences were deleted it would be reduced to a pamphlet.

As this is written, *The World of Suzie Wong* is the latest addition to the whore-lore to be hailed for its ineffable warmth and charm. Its Asiatic locale lends it something of the One World or UN touch.

A doctoral thesis is waiting to come from the ranks of the academic critics on "The Madam as Philosopher." She has shoved the bartender right out of the act. Sinclair Lewis said the American ideal was the great sales manager. Now it is in a fair way to becoming the great brothel keeper, if we are to believe what we read.

It would take a book much bigger than this one, and it would require a clinically trained man, to analyze fully the motivation behind the whorehouse mystique. My only speculations are that it arises in part out of that same immaturity discussed above, which seeks a frankly transitory and limited relationship, fleeing from permanence or responsibility, including the responsibility of giving satisfaction to the female partner. It implies, too, a refuge of moral anarchy, since it is the peculiarity of our mores to regard the prostitute as inherently inferior to her customer. Again, it implies an arena where inhibition can vanish, where one can do anything because there is no one there whose judgment counts. Moreover, the madam, or the whore herself, is supposed to be all-knowing about the needs and weaknesses of the male.

Also, the whore is imagined (with rather sweeping optimism) to be the ultimate erotic technician (again relieving the male of any obligations but guaranteeing his good time). That this could be equated with passionate responsiveness is one of the greatest evidences of the utter unreality of the concept of whoredom which these novels celebrate.

Whether in or out of the brothel, many of our writers, possibly in response to an inner fear of their own private inability to arouse, depict for us zombie women of the most avid and voracious lubricity. These ladies of perpetual heat, these creatures of the night-sweat and wet dream, are no more than literary succubi, erotic hauntings. We see glimpses of this imaginary shadowland of panting, insatiable, eager female flesh in the late John Horne Burns' *A Cry of Children* (which would be a good collective title for the total work of many writers), in which his lecherous and ill-smelling apartment house landlord, Mr. Kubelik, caressingly characterized, brags of his many women who mind neither his dirt nor odor:

> Dey know I'm tirty but dey like vat I'ff got to offer. No American man haff it any more. Maybe dey vunce had it, in de time of Jefferson, but dey lost sometink. Nowadays many American men prefer vun anudder, and dere

vimmin haff driven em to it, maybe. Ah, vat a
country, vat a country. . . . Almost all cas-
trated or Lesbian, but vat fun and vat money!

But we couldn't even begin an exploration of the
whorehouse in fiction without one of the best-known
theorizers about our sex life, Mr. Philip Wylie, America's number one cocktail-party-style philosopher, anti-
Momist, and self-appointed devil's advocate. He has
skill, articulateness, and the ability to arouse and hold
interest when he starts to address almost any subject,
but then has nowhere to go with it. His specialized
novel, *Tomorrow*, written as civil defense propaganda,
reveals his first-class gifts as a science-fiction writer,
and is superb when describing the destruction of cities
in nuclear war, yet its civil defense message is be-
fogged by the sophomoric philosophizing of minor-
Bob-Ingersoll vintage gratuitously injected into it.

As a high-school boy I read his *Finnley Wren* and
was swept off my feet by it, feeling that this was the
voice of the new enlightenment. In rereading *Finnley
Wren*, and most of what Wylie has written since, I've
been forced into the feeling that I've grown up meanwhile and that he hasn't.

He is a moralist after his own fashion. He castigates
his kind of sinners much as the Devil might—in con-
tempt for their behavior but in defiance of a moral law.
He hates any profession of a moral law one shade more
than he hates misdeeds. In *Generation of Vipers* and
An Essay on Morals he is a two-bit, inverted Jeremiah,
touching real abuses in our culture but twisting his
attack upon the very sources of that culture.

His view of the condition of many American males is not unlike that of the above-quoted Mr. Kubelik, but the full range of his ideas is much more sweeping. His theories of sex antedate Kinsey, yet he seized upon Kinsey, opportunistically, accepting his statistics uncritically, which is more than the trained analyst of statistical procedures is prepared to do. However, the statistical question can be put aside here, for I agree with Wylie on one aspect of his response to the Reports. I, like Wylie, had studied these behavior phenomena in Freud, Krafft-Ebing, Stekel, and Ellis, and I, like Wylie, had recognized their traces in my own buried impulses. The widespread incidence of such phenomena as the late Dr. Kinsey reports came as no surprise to anyone reasonably versed in the history of psychiatry, in anthropology, in classical literature, in moral theology, or in simple self-knowledge.

The question is, What of it? Wylie is of that school which argues that if people do a thing it should be done. To him, Kinsey has proved that "the sexual behavior of people is mammalian in every respect. . . . We behave sexually like other mammals—apes, horses, dogs." It is quite true that we are mammals and that we share some of the basic sexual characteristics, impulses, or instincts of our mammalian kin. Yet it does not seem to suggest itself to Wylie that we are unique among mammals, that we differ from all others, from whale to wolf, and that the essential nature of that difference, which lies in the fact of self-consciousness, necessarily invalidates and makes absurd glib generalizations about man's sexual adjustment by simple analogy to that of the stoat or the housecat. The fundamental facts that our processes of sexual selection are so much more complex, that we are conscious of individual personality, that we are conscious of the fact that we procreate our species, and that we have no automatic mating season are enough to invalidate the simple mammalian analogy as a guide to our standard for human sexual behavior.

I haven't read anything like Wylie's sexual and marital theories since early Dora and Bertrand Russell. He is totally permissive in the sexual realm, urging in the name of health, for the purging of what he calls our neurotic, Christian-rooted sexual sickness, the uninhibited yielding to every sexual impulse, in childhood or adulthood, pre-marital or extra-marital, heterosexual or homosexual, short of an open tangle with the law.

These ideas permeate his work in general, but specifically, for present purposes, are derived from one book in particular, the odd, interesting, and frenetic novel called *Opus 21*, which is greatly germane to our discussion. In it Philip Wylie is protagonist and narrator, in his own proper person, thus giving maximum range to his strident polemics.

His immense reserves of sexual-social-scientific wisdom are expended lavishly in *Opus 21*, and I'm interested in the devices of his revelation. He picks up in a bar a nice blonde named Yvonne, who is reading the Kinsey Report under a phony wrapper. She has fled from her husband, mightily upset, because she had caught him in a homosexual act in a greenhouse. By the end of the book, after a lot of talk with Wylie, and a few rounds of personal experimentation with a friendly whore she meets in his apartment and hijacks, Yvonne is on her feet again, all straightened out and on her way back to her husband, explaining, "Because—Rol—me, too!"

As a subplot, we have the absorbing story of his nephew, Paul, a young nuclear physicist, who arrives at Uncle Phil's apartment one day, obviously under stress. The trouble is blurted out in a few moments, in the now classical terms of the great whorehouse tradition. Right in the middle of *Opus 21* we meet Gambit 21: "I'm in love. And the girl's a whore." Unlike Jones' Lorene, this one is the well-groomed, high-level callgirl type. The house, in and out of which she works, is more like one of Polly Adler's than Mrs. Kipfer's. Wylie takes us there to meet his old friend (and ours) the philosopher-madam, named Hattie.

"If people only knew what I know!" Hattie says. ". . . It'll take thousands of years. . . . They've been making the same mistakes, that long." (". . . There were tears not only in her eyes but on her cheeks.")

While Hattie is generalizing about the problem of Paul and Marcia, she sounds another familiar note: "Some of them make damned good wives—better sometimes for being here. With the kind of men who really understand what life is. . . . There are worse places to look for a wife than good bagnios. Any high society party, for instance. Women's colleges, too . . ."

Hattie has words, also, on the sexual incompetence of the American wife. "Did you ever," she demands of Phil, "ever once have an affair with a plain American wife who was any good? Somebody else's, I mean? . . . I've had lots of men bring their wives right here —to look and learn . . . many a snooty female has lost her inhibitions in my parlors—and gained a little knowledge that went into making a happy home for some guy."

When *Opus 21* appeared in 1949, intelligent reviewers gave it solemn attention, Diana Trilling noting its "basic perception about the sexual nature of our ills," and William Targ speaking of its "devastating entertainment and enlightenment."

Thus Wylie's blueprint to save the world (in this book) presents his credentials as universal moral revisionist, and super-expert at large. He is the most all-encompassing master mind since da Vinci (or Shaw, who knew better how to do the pitch). He knows more psychology than Freud, more physics than Fermi, more theology than the Pope, and cheerfully tells off the waiting world in any realm of competence. Psychology, he assures us, has utterly voided every aspect of our sex mores; psychology and physics have demolished all religion. His half-baked scraps of scientific jargons glitter dazzlingly in the advanced hours of cocktail parties but fade into tedious puerility on the printed page.

If, in this sea of sweeping pronouncements, Wylie invents a nuclear physicist who falls in love with a whore, I know a real nuclear physicist who became an Episcopal priest; I can point to a Freudian psychoanalyst, writer, and teacher of analysts, who is a

Roman Catholic; and there are many comparable instances. The naïveté and childishness of his glib assumptions and the scratchy old records of both plot
and debate in *Opus 21* simply show us that as an intellectual and social commentator, Wylie is right up
there with the front runners of the nineteenth century.

Wylie's view of man is simple and modest. Man is
God—affirmed in *Opus 21* and reaffirmed in his later
novel, *The Disappearance*, and present in slightly more
subdued tones in his most recent non-fiction, *The Innocent Ambassadors*. The mess that man is in is due
to religion, and religious-inspired sexual repression.
This minister's son is a fanatical anti-Christian, ranging
far out of his stride for any sideswipe at Christianity
and Christians. Upon Christianity he pours the onus of
total responsibility for all the viciousness, hypocrisy,
prudery, cynicism, brutality, and avarice that scourge
the world (and in the guilt of which Christian men and
Christian institutions indeed are inextricably involved).
But Wylie, the enlightened prophet, free of it all, will
show the way. *Opus 21* is part of his chart.

In many ponderous and portentous books, modern
woman has been discussed in terms ranging from the
"lost sex" to the "second sex." She has emerged from
the early political-economic battles of the suffrage
movement more or less victorious, taking her place
honorably and effectively in many aspects of public
and professional life once closed to her. Now she is
conscious of herself and the subtler dilemmas of her
nature and social role more than in any earlier age.

She is torn among a variety of needs and wishes and drives, all natural to her, all representing rightful areas of fulfillment and experience, but terribly difficult to relate or hold together in a single, practical pattern of life. She still feels forced to select some, and reject other, expressions and experiences in kinds of choices that her male partner is less generally compelled to make. She desires to be both female and feminine in love, to be desirable, to have a happy marriage and to bear children, to find in her husband a masculine strength which she can respect and upon which she can depend, to make a home and to be a helpmate. But she may desire, without relinquishing these rights, also to be a doctor, a businesswoman, a senator, an artist of a variety of kinds, a physicist, a professor, a grade-school teacher, or an executive. Less formally, she may simply desire opportunities for exploration of herself as a person, an entity, an intellect. Can she do these things, be these things, and be still a man's wife and lover, a bearer of children and a nurturing mother? Her problem—a hard one no less than midway, if that far, toward solution—is how to be a man's mate without being his satellite, or how to be an entity in her own right without being unsexed.

The male, of course, has his problems when confronted with this new seeking and demanding woman. The challenge she offers to the male has made a rich field for the psychoanalyst—as has the challenge she offers to herself. The sheer competition with this woman, in professional or personal terms, may undermine male security and arouse inferiority feelings. It contributes to the rise of homosexuality (a problem which, while real, I believe to be exaggerated in terms of emphasis in our literature) and to what has been called, more broadly, a "retreat from masculinity."

Indeed, the woman even partly self-realized as a true person rather than as a type of her sex, is by no means easy for a man to cope with, either maritally or in any other relationship. One can imagine the secret cry: "If women are going to be *persons* it isn't worth while to be men." The adaptation to a "separate but equal" sex seems too difficult to some men. In fleeing the difficulties of this adaptation they have fled the rewards of it —which are great.

The male reactions and perplexities are reflected in fiction in a wide variety of ways. Frank Hirsh, the hero's brother, in Jones' *Some Came Running*, broods about women: ". . . He could not get over this feeling he had that something was happening to American women anymore. Something bad. They weren't even *women* anymore. They were *men*. . . . They didn't act like women are supposed to act."

Some novelists, consciously or otherwise, are avenging themselves upon women, degrading and humiliating them vicariously, triumphing over them in a fictional domination, sexual and otherwise, that is lost from their life reality. Other writers, less disturbed, cling nevertheless to the picture of woman as an appendage to man and a sexual object, rather than attempt to deal in fiction with the emergent woman so perplexing to deal with in life. The yearning for a pattern of relationship strictly as it used to be (or more so) is reflected in the love and marriage relationships of GIs in parts of Europe, but especially in Asia, where the position of woman still remains clearly subordinate and she dances at man's beck and call and defers to his wishes. The back-scrubbing, bed-warming simple woman, as set forth by Michener in *Sayonara*, expresses a lingering male ideal: the female satellite, orbiting around the male, adaptive to his moods, sexually assuaging, cocoon-spinning, and above all, isolated from his other, outer, male world of activities.

There is a tremendous lag, in literature, behind the vanguard of men and women valiantly striving to know each other more excitingly in a greater sharing of mind and body as equal persons. I have yet to see a fully conscious or deeply probing attempt at drawing the emergent woman and the new kinds of relationships possible, and necessary, with her. That such studies will begin to appear in novels, from both men and women, and will advance in depth and excitement, is a certainty. I look forward to their appearance with as much excitement as I look toward the apparently more imminent landings on the moon.

Meanwhile, our best writers, who are not generally those in the foreground with new blasts of violent sensationalism, are those men and women alike who, far from resolving the yet unresolved questions about woman, yet approach the characterization of women, or of men, in the effort to see distinguishable individuals, independent personal entities. To represent both sexes, the novels of Nancy Wilson Ross and of James Gould Cozzens are good examples of the general attempt to see individuals as such. The grotesque and immature conceptions of sexual relationships that I have sketched in this chapter do not occur in the books of such mature and thoughtful writers, even though all the complexities and problems and errors and sicknesses of sexual relations may be studied in them. Some vision, at least, of a possible rational and humane sexual relationship undergirds them.

There are two great facets of sex in the life of man. It is both unitive and procreative—and it is these things above and beyond anything else that can be made of it. The radical disorders of the sexual life to which all of us are variously liable, and to which it is true that errors of the religious and moral sense often contribute, can at their extreme make of sex something divisive and fruitless—the complete thwarting of its two supreme functions. But we are confronted with writers who do not know these functions, or do not believe in them, or who reject them. They show us the symptoms or last states of disordered sexuality and say that this is indeed the nature of the sexuality of man. My quarrel, again, is not against portraying the disorder—it is against failing to recognize the disorder for what it is and failing to have some vision or concept of a proper state for man's sexuality. No rational conception of such a proper state, of course, implies perfection, for nothing of man's life is perfection.

None of the harsh, tough novelists comprehend in any way the bearing of children as the fruition and fulfillment of love. The concept is alien to them. I have spoken of "non-fertility rites." Typically, James Jones' Dave Hirsh, when he marries, reflects: "Thank God, at least, they didn't have to worry about having any damned kids, too; Ginnie's gonorrhea when she was a kid had made her sterile, so at least they didn't have to worry about that, thank God." Could they have had children they would have been damned kids indeed.

The awe, mystery, and wonder of birth are celebrated uniquely and sometimes tragically in the late Morton Thompson's *The Cry and the Covenant*, which should be read by everyone who has had, or hopes to have, a child. And the nature of love as fulfilled in family is perceived deeply in the late James Agee's tender and beautiful *A Death in the Family*.

In one of his novels, Charles Williams says of a woman: "She had the common, vague idea of her age that if your sexual life was all right you were all right, and she had the common vague idea of all ages that if you (and your sexual life) were not all right, it was probably someone else's fault." This simplification of problems, and this incorrigible impulse to shift responsibility, color much fiction.

D. H. Lawrence, in the preface to one edition of the unbowdlerized *Lady Chatterley's Lover*, suggested that if the world would resume the free, uninhibited use of the Anglo-Saxon monosyllables relating to elimination and copulation, all our neuroses would melt away. There is much charm in this simple doctrine. Its only drawback is that it isn't true, though some novelists are doing their best to advance it. There may be more of a home truth in the shrewd observation of C. S. Lewis in his book, *Mere Christianity:*

> They tell you sex has become a mess because it was hushed up. But for the last twenty years it has not been hushed up. It has been chattered about all day long. Yet it is still in a mess. If hushing up had been the cause of the trouble, ventilation would have set it right. But it has not. I think it is the other way round. I think the human race originally hushed it up because it had become such a mess. Modern people are always saying, "Sex is nothing to be ashamed of." They may mean two things. They may mean "There is nothing to be ashamed of in the fact that the human race reproduces itself in a certain way, nor in the fact that it gives pleasure." If they mean that, they are right.

A novelist told me some years ago that a forthcoming book of his had as one of its messages the fact that "sex can be fun." This I am not able to buy—not because I would deny the pleasures of sex, but because I find the term inadequate. Fun is not a large enough word for what is to be realized in sex. Too many commonplaces are fun; for sex nothing short of ecstasy will do. Sex, in fulfillment, is not fun, but is ecstatic, a condition of exaltation and pleasure at the threshold of pain, so that conversely sex without a true union and fulfillment can be at the least a desolation and at the worst an agony and anguish.

Since I set forth an objection to the notion of sex as fun, I should append a word on the question of whether sex can be funny. Of course it can. In both novels and plays the sex farce, or satire, is a long-standing and honorable institution, from *Lysistrata* through *Joseph Andrews* to *Will Success Spoil Rock Hunter?*

Man's often grotesque or ludicrous concupiscence, like all other of man's vices and follies, is the legitimate subject of farce and satire. The source of the laughter is not the particular manifestation itself, but the folly. Sex certainly is one of the universal areas in which man is betrayed into making a fool of himself. Man's ability to laugh at his folly is indirectly an affirmation of a value. Steve Allen has said wisely, "Things are funny in some sort of loose relation to how far they fall short of perfection." And Hazlitt, before him, had said, "Man is the only animal that laughs and weeps; for he is the only animal that is struck with the difference between what things are, and what they ought to be."

Farce is wholesome when it portrays folly identified as folly. It is when folly is unrecognized and passed off as truth or reality that it becomes a grievous matter.

Sex is not a means of self-obliteration, though it is sometimes used as such. It is, through union with a beloved, the vehicle of the greatest self-knowledge through the uniting knowledge of the partner. It is not a monologue, it is a dialogue, as is every level of actual living.

One of the small, profound books of our age is the Jewish philosopher Martin Buber's *I and Thou*. Buber is the great exponent of the life of dialogue. The condition in which an *I* knows in full consciousness its relation with a *Thou* is a true dialogue, a true human encounter, at any level or with any being. This is rarer than we think. Many of our relationships, even with people, are at the level merely of *I-It*. This is always a subhuman relationship. In sexual terms it is the transaction between a man and a prostitute, Philip Wylie notwithstanding, or between any two persons to either or both of whom the other stands as object; it is what happens between user and used. A matured and fulfilled sexual bond is an *I-Thou* relationship.

In the books of many current novelists no relationships are seen at this level—it is as if the knowledge of the very existence of the level were lacking, as perhaps it is. Women, in these books, find no true existence as human, individual entities. They are vessels for male use. It is assumed that man is a person and woman a receptacle. It would be one thing if the tragedy of such an estate or the circumstances of arriving at it were the subjects of books. It is not that some men do not treat women as mere objects, for alas they do. My complaint is at the picture of a world in which this is conceived as the true role of woman and the reality of man's sexuality. A writer who himself holds this concept, or who can see and portray no other, may be able to accomplish various things, but he will never be able to paint for us the living portrait of a woman, or to project a true and total union between a man and his mate.

8

Joyce: Dedalus or Icarus?

The problem of Joyce confronts every modern writer and critic. The body of discussion about him is so large that I have little impulse to add to it. Most of the Joyce debate has been either on the rarefied esthetic level, in which interpreters of *Finnegans Wake* rebuke each other for their gross errors, or has been *ad hominum* from those who, like Gogarty, say in effect, "I knew him *when* and I can tell you the real truth about him." The little that I wish to say is specifically concerned with his image of man.

Let me make the preliminary concessions briefly. True, Joyce possessed a kind of genius, or near-genius. He pioneered, with both good and bad results, the post-Freudian approach to characterization. He introduced new ways of telling a story, most notably his development of the interior monologue and "stream of consciousness" as modes of advancing a narrative. Again, for both good and bad, he has influenced the way in which many novelists since him have written their books. He possessed massive scholarship and exceptional linguistic gifts. His works have a kind of maniacal brilliance . . .

. . . but, as a conception of man in his nature and life, like John Randolph's famous rotten mackerel in the moonlight, they shine and stink. A derisive distaste for man, self and other than self, permeates them. They culminate in a gigantic mockery, conscious and controlled on the artistic level, but less so, I think, in their sources and motivation. The Joyce cultists insist that *Ulysses* and *Finnegans Wake* are "genial," humor-filled books, but their grin is a *risus sardonicus*. They are, Gogarty claims, "a gigantic hoax, one of the most enormous leg-pulls in history." It is a claim that need not be settled for the purposes of this discussion.

Certainly the influence of Joyce has been at least partly baleful. So powerful a radiation as that emitted by his decay could not fail to have effects. His ingenious skills and the obscurantism of the two late books have hypnotized many susceptibles into acceptance of not just a technical but a philosophical package that a lesser man could not have peddled with comparable success. His work and the passionate cult developed around it have, in Gogarty's words, presented "boredom, dirt, and despair as fitting subjects for poetry and prose." Also, "They ask us to bow down before all followers of 'The Master.' . . . They ask us to join them in hailing the loss of human dignity, the degradation and disgrace of Man."

Joyce has been elevated into a figure who has been seized upon by many writers as inspiration and justification for that whole wing of fiction and drama that has repudiated man and extolled unman. That is the truest sense in which he is the founder of a movement.

Few men have said more eloquent things about art, beauty, and the special dedications of the artist than some of the lines in *A Portrait of the Artist as a Young Man*. It is to the priesthood of art and the esthetic that Stephen dedicates himself, in terms of his namesake, Dedalus, the "old artificer," not an artist but the inventor of wings. The philosophic pitfall is in the glib assumption that devotion to art is a dedication to a religion not capable of coexistence or reconciliation with any other religion—an assumption which overlooks or would negate an immense volume of humanity's greatest artistic achievements in every field. Actually, the religion that Stephen embraces is not at all a religion of art—it is a religion of Man. The premise of this remarkable novel seems to be that man, to fulfill himself, must worship his own creativity, and that to worship God is to deny himself. "*Non serviam*": this is Dedalus-Joyce's great discovery and "liberation."

It is a large boast for a man to say he has overreached the medium of his species' linguistic resources. No other man in literature has found that existing language and syntax could not contain him in its constructions and vocabularies. Saying, with Stephen, that he will "fly by those nets" of "nationality, language, religion," that he requires "a new terminology," Joyce went totally into the world of the private communication, the world of talking to oneself.

Now what is the nature of Joyce's concepts, of his vision and understanding of life, which compels him to reject as an inadequate vehicle the previous media and modes of communication? *Ulysses* and *Finnegans Wake* are remarkable technical and intellectual performances. What is in them? What is claimed for them?

This high priest of man portrays demented man. Joyce has created a religion with an insane god. The obscene eucharist celebrated in the brothel scene of *Ulysses* is its expression. The image of man visible in Joyce had been sketched graphically before his time in the Fantasies of Peter Breughel and in the Capriccios of Goya. They harmonize perfectly with the famous scene in Bella Cohen's brothel, or the Molly Bloom interior monologue, in *Ulysses,* as well as with *Finnegans Wake.* Both Breughel and Goya castigated in nightmare fury the sometime malignancy and viciousness of man. Joyce accepts these grotesques in broad daylight with the mocking pretension that they are the lords of creation. The affirmation that there is nothing greater than these creatures in the universe is seen by Joyce not as a source of anger or of pride, but of derisive laughter.

I want to consider Joyce together with a reputable spokesman for his cult. As such I choose the little book, admirable upon its own premises, by W. Y. Tindall, *James Joyce; His Way of Interpreting the Modern World.* It is precisely this subtitle with which I am concerned, for it is simply another way of saying his view of modern man.

In Joyce's cosmos, as Tindall explains, "Man would do tolerably well for God; but to replace Christianity Joyce needed a system in which man could occupy the center." But as hinted a moment ago, this is not a triumphant, optimistic, song-of-progress mood. Joyce represents a sharp swing, remarkably early, toward the disillusioned reverse of the cult of triumphant Man, out of which comes so much pustular contemporary literature. To cite Tindall again: "As if a humanist, Joyce placed man at the center; but he rejected progress and retained original sin. His vision is one of imperfect men falling and rising *to no end*." (My italics.)

Joyce's interpretation and creation of human character, vivid and perceptive, has as its basis and rationale "—all the machinery of Freud, incredibly enlarged and multiplied—" (and prematurely and uncritically accepted). The irony is that Joyce, whose rebellion was in the name of individuality, who is acclaimed by his admirers as a prophet of individuality, through his crudely literal early-Freudianism stepped onto the path that leads to the death of the individual, submerging him in bestiality and determinism, which we see graphically in much of the contemporary fiction, triple-fathered (like one of Shaw's characters) by Marx, Freud, and Joyce.

The mire in *Ulysses* and *Finnegans Wake* should be regarded beside the pretensions of the works. (Let us dismiss any questions of pornography, as Judge Woolsey properly did in his historic decision lifting the ban from *Ulysses*.) Tindall assures us that Joyce's "formal vision, uniting our intellectual and aesthetic interests, presents all our reality. . . . As *Finnegans Wake* is the total reality of night, *Ulysses* is the total reality of day."

This purported total reality is above all things pre-occupied with the Freudian sexual symbols and the grosser bodily functions. The mind and creativity of man presumably are celebrated in *A Portrait of the Artist,* but only in the limited terms of Stephen's esoteric estheticism. The spiritual life of man is repre-sented only in the obscenities of the later books, the grotesque, mockingly blasphemous parodies of liturgy and creed which dominate both big volumes. These reveal Joyce thrashing in convulsions at the end of his unsevered Roman Catholic umbilical cord. In spite of his repudiation of his faith and tradition, he tied himself to it by abuse.

Then we find extraordinary equations which Joyce and his interpreters insist upon. Thus, in some places, H. C. Earwicker is God. Leopold Bloom is equated at times with Christ, Elijah, and Moses, in a mood of farce, as in the celebrated ascension or apotheosis:

> And there came a voice out of heaven, call-ing: *Elijah! Elijah!* And he answered with a main cry: *Abba! Adonai!* And they beheld Him even Him, ben Bloom Elijah, amid clouds of angels ascend to the glory of the brightness at an angle of forty-five degrees over Dono-hoe's in Little Green Street like a shot off a shovel.

Tindall solemnly tells us: "To Joyce's way of thinking, not even Jesus, with whom Bloom is compared, approaches the humanity of Bloom."

Similarly, Molly Bloom, that lady of perpetual heat, is sometimes equated with the Virgin, sometimes with the ancient, Mediterranean Great Mother. As to her weight in the book, Tindall observes that "Compared to her, nothing seems very important." He describes the last two pages of her famous interior monologue that ends the book as "a hymn to God and nature," on the basis of a few lines of tritely idiotic sentimentality by Molly about roses and mountains. The grossness of this exaggeration of value and disregard of context is readily seen if the experimenter will check the last four pages instead.

Bloom, the critic tells us, "is every man in our time." On an enlarged scale, H. C. Earwicker, of *Finnegans Wake*, "is every man in history. His initials produce *Here Comes Everybody*." The book employs the device of "a night's sleep to represent the nature and condition of man." We are further assured that "*Finnegans Wake* is a symbol of eternity," followed up with the text from the holy writing itself: "In the buginning was the woid."

We are coming squarely home to the point. If the nature and condition of man are as represented in *Ulysses* and *Finnegans Wake*, then indeed Joyce is all that his cult elevates him to be. If the nature and condition of man are not as represented in these two books, then they become curious phenomena, not without worth and significance by any means, but products of a warped and derisive gift. Their unchallengeable importance is as specimens of the product of just such a view of man as they embody. Their existence, and even more so the existence of the almost priestly cult attached to them, are contemporary phenomena of great import.

We see, here, the absolute difficulty. Judgment of Joyce is a matter of premise. The opinions of a Joyce cultist and a non-cultist are irreconcilable. The same texts will be cited, between them, to prove diametrically contrary points.

Meanwhile, the growing body of Joycean exegesis confronts us with material which comes close to parodying itself to any reader not wholly under the spell. For example, we have Tindall, on the meaning of a passage involving some girls in the Park (Eden) in which Earwicker has committed some "unclear" sin:

> Innumerable hints make it certain that the girls are relieving themselves. Earwicker, observing them, is either a voyeur, as psychoanalysts know the peeper, or else an exhibitionist. The soldiers meanwhile are observing him. Maybe he makes improper advances to the soldiers or maybe the whole scandal, as the work of gossips, is without foundation. All this is so obscure that even an experienced reader is apt to go astray. One commentator, for example, thinks a certain passage describes a body washing about in the surf. To be sure there is "A thud of surf," but it is heard

through "minxmingled hair." Attention to the
Latin pun in its context identifies the theme
as two girls making water in the bushes.

Prior to this notable specimen (I choose my word
carefully) of "explication of the text," as the process
is called in the higher criticism, Tindall has conceded
one of the Master's recurrent preoccupations:

> It cannot be denied that in *Chamber Music*
> and *Finnegans Wake* Joyce seems devoted to
> urination. Most men retain something infan-
> tile; and all men, the analysts assure us, are
> either anal or oral in character. But those of
> the anal type are better stylists.

A point of equal interest is to be found in Edmund
Wilson's *New Yorker* review, in 1944, of the Joseph
Campbell-Henry Morton Robinson *A Skeleton Key to
Finnegans Wake*. Wilson observes that Joyce's book
"has acquired the reputation of being inordinately difficult to read." He doesn't think it's really so difficult.
Still, he welcomes the Campbell-Robinson *Key* and
praises it highly as having "opened up the book to the
public at the cost of much patience and care."

Still, Mr. Wilson gives them a rap on the knuckles
for at least one unpardonable error:

> . . . They seem to think that Earwicker,
> through part of the book, has been lying drunk
> on the floor of the pub, and that he goes up-
> stairs to bed at some point, and that later, in
> the scene before dawn, when one of the twins

wakes the mother and she goes into his room to calm him, the husband really goes in with her and afterwards has intercourse with her, whereas it is plain that, in the first case, the falling on the floor and the going upstairs themselves take place in the dream and that, in the second, he has hardly awakened but, half aware of what his wife is doing, has sunk back into fitful slumber. It is an essential feature of the plan of the book, it makes its artistic unity, that Earwicker shall be always in bed and that he shall never wake up till morning—just the moment after the book ends. The later chapters of the "Skeleton Key" are thus definitely unsatisfactory.

Such sober-sided unconscious parodies of exegesis can be duplicated extensively from the literature on Joyce. What is the sum total after the playing of these elaborate games of cryptography and exposition?

We have a body of work venerated by its adherents as Holy Writ. The names of Dante and Milton are most commonly advanced as comparisons notwithstanding that both gentlemen wrote their languages intelligibly and offer a somewhat different view of man. In spite of the accolades heaped on Joyce as a master of English prose (which indeed he was when he wished to be), the two chief works are written, one partly and the other entirely, in a jargon that prevents them from being read intelligibly without years of study and the use of guides. We find the priests who prepare the guides spitting at one another, from time to time, over alleged misreadings.

These works have been called obscene and indecent. This aspect has been disposed of definitively by Judge Woolsey in his well-known observation that while in parts *Ulysses* "undoubtedly is somewhat emetic, nowhere does it tend to be an aphrodisiac."

Some have insisted that the books are a vast and malicious jest—a hoax. This is perhaps inadequate, as an explanation of them, although I do not think Mr. Gogarty's observations about Joyce, from his first-hand knowledge of both the man and the Dublin background, can be dismissed without careful attention.

I share some of the cult's admiration for the sheer ingenuity seen in the books. But I think that the world of Joyce is a world of stink and death. I think that Joyce saw it exactly as he set it down. And I think that his body of work together with the body of exegesis that has sprung up around it are a perfect and terrifying example of the disintegrative process in the mind that has pinned its utter faith upon its own intellectual, rational, and creative powers to the exclusion of all else.

Joyce insisted upon regarding man as *prime creator* instead of accepting him as that quite sufficient marvel: *creative creature.* He cast himself as Dedalus the "artificer." Perhaps he is more that rash son of Dedalus, that Icarus, who, against the counsel of the artificer, flew too near the sun on wings he had not made.

9

The hipster or the organization man?

There is certainly some truth in John Aldridge's contention that ours is a period particularly marked by conformity to our standards of mass culture and mass behavior. William H. Whyte, Jr., has explored brilliantly the current cultus of what he has dubbed "the organization man." At the same time, none of the examinations of the problem, from Mr. Aldridge's perspective in literary criticism to Mr. Whyte's sociology or cultural anthropology, succeeds in the difficult task of drawing a line between conformity to "crowd culture," as B. I. Bell calls it, and identification with some form of rational and systematic living.

Since writers tend to portray life at its dramatic extremes rather than on its median ground, we could get the impression from reading both contemporary fiction and non-fiction, that the choice of behavior paths currently available to man lies between the organization man and what has come to be known as the "hipster."

I am greatly concerned over the question of whether these represent valid alternatives.

Probably the foremost prophet of hipsterism is Jack Kerouac, and an item of its holy writ is his novel, *On the Road*, which was published in the fall of 1957 and received a large measure of critical attention. Such significance as it has surely is that of one pattern of revolt against the "square" world, which may be interpreted either as the world of conformity, or simply the world of rational and responsible living. In the lexicon of Mr. Kerouac, and even, as we have seen earlier, in the lexicon of so different a man as Mr. Aldridge, the two are frequently blurred or fused together.

Perhaps we can view this problem, or these alternatives, with reasonable rewards, by examining two books, which either are, or have been considered to be, representations of the extremes: Herman Wouk's *The Caine Mutiny* and Jack Kerouac's *On the Road*.

The Caine Mutiny is one of the biggest best sellers of recent years. A number of critics or social analysts, most notably John Aldridge, William H. Whyte, Jr., Harvey Swados, and Martin Dworkin, have attempted to read into this enormous popularity the implication that it is because the vision or ideal of behavior projected in the book is supremely that of the contemporary conformist or organization man.

In the first place, there is something unsound in the attempt to find a connection between the extensive sale of the book and some particular *zeitgeist*, or pattern of the age. How does this assumption as applied to *The*

Caine Mutiny jibe with the also enormous sales of *From Here to Eternity* and *The Naked and the Dead,* or the positively staggering sales of the collected works of Mickey Spillane? Are we to assume that in the case of Wouk we can see a response to the portrayal of the ideal of conformity, any more than we would see in the response to Jones, Mailer, or Spillane the acceptance of some ideal of conduct? Far too much is built upon the circumstance of popularity. It may well be that there are partial truths in some of the contentions made about the view of life in *The Caine Mutiny,* and in the claim that this view has contributed to its popularity, but there are also substantial and adequate other reasons contributing to its popularity as a book, a play, and a film, not the least of which is the simple fact that it's a good story.

It seems to me that Mr. Wouk has been the victim of an unusual amount of unfair criticism. I think much of this is due to the book's considerable contrast to the view of life and behavior reflected in *The Naked and the Dead* and *From Here to Eternity,* which have been accepted far too readily as valid or normative views of the behavior and attitudes of man, particularly within the framework of the military experience. Because the Mailer and Jones books received rather more credit than can be considered their due, and because *The Caine Mutiny* stood in such marked contrast to them, there has been a tendency in those who boosted the former to make the contrast of the latter a fault in itself. Accordingly, the onus that the critics occasionally heap upon the circumstance of being a best seller, from which the Jones and Mailer books were exempted, was heaped unsparingly upon the head of Mr. Wouk.

Now let us sum up the attack on *The Caine Mutiny*. Mr. Aldridge refers the case to Harvey Swados' "devastating *Partisan Review* essay" which "rendered superflous all further efforts to pin down the causes both of Mr. Wouk's peculiar offensiveness in the novel and his remarkable public popularity—the two being, as Mr. Swados shows, quite obviously identical."

Again: ". . . The *Caine Mutiny* audience was allowed to participate vicariously in both defiance of established authority—the relieving of Queeg—and a concluding affirmation of its necessity—the defense of Queeg—"

Martin Dworkin, in reviewing the play, *The Caine Mutiny Court-Martial*, reached the conclusion that "Wouk wants us to think less and obey more."

But I think the most interesting and direct charge against Wouk is summed up in that chapter from Whyte's *The Organization Man* which is called "Love That System." After considering Maryk's action in relieving Queeg, and after considering the complexities involved in the action which are developed in the course of the court-martial, and after considering the outcome of the trial and the celebrated cocktail-party defense of Queeg which Greenwald makes, Whyte assumes that for the book as a whole "the lesson is plain. It is not for the individual to question the system."

All the critics are making a highly selective, card-stacked approach to the book. They are omitting to give proper weight to one essential element in its context, and are further ignoring other aspects of the story and its characters.

All these critics are either ignoring or slurring over the absolutely vital fact that the events of this book take place not in society at large but within that highly specialized closed system, a military establishment. The whole question of authority and the individual within the military closed system is, has been from time immemorial, and will continue to be, a specialized one from which we cannot generalize and draw analogies relative to non-military society.

One of the distinguishing characteristics of *The Caine Mutiny* was its ability to view the problem within the inescapable military premise without oversimplifying it. Mr. Wouk does not relate the central situations of *The Caine Mutiny* to civilian life at large, and it is not fair of his critics to assume that he has done so, or to attempt to do so themselves. Sloan Wilson's *The Man in the Grey Flannel Suit*, which John Aldridge links with *The Caine Mutiny*, is in a wholly different genre and context altogether, and cannot be bracketed with the Wouk book. I would not wish to rise to the defense of Mr. Wilson's singularly unexciting novel, against which the objectors have a strong case. It deals with situations in civilian hierarchies of authority. It poses its moral challenges and their solutions in terms of popular liberal clichés, artificial and oversimplified, but highly palatable to the *lumpen* middle class.

If the Maryk-Queeg dilemma, and all that flowed from it, were occurring in the context of a civilian business or industrial hierarchy; if it were the revolt of a young executive against the general manager or the president, with the issue being referred for decision to the board of directors in lieu of a court-martial—the criticisms of Wouk's detractors would have more validity. But this is not the context of *The Caine Mutiny*.

Maryk does act to supersede Queeg, knowing that, regardless of the outcome, it cannot be a simple question of black and white, and is bound to cause trouble for him. The reader, too, is aware of this but cannot anticipate all the complexities which the trial brings forward. It is quite true that the *Caine* was wallowing; it is quite true that she subsequently passed a bottoms-up destroyer which may have been following the tactics of Queeg (under some other skipper whom no one argues to have been insane). All the same, it cannot be proved that had Maryk not acted, the *Caine* definitely would have foundered. Wouk does not make such an assertion. This is true to the basic life situation insofar as major decisions, fraught with dire personal consequences, often must be made without any positive certainty that the action involved is absolutely necessary, or that its alternatives would be surely disastrous. Life would be a simple and happy proposition indeed if conclusions could be reached with such certainty, either before events or by hindsight. This is part of the subtlety and complexity of the dilemma.

It is an oversimplification to say that Maryk is permitted to defy authority and is then slapped over the wrist for the defiance. And again this ignores the special context of the military situation. It is quite true that Article 184 in the Naval Regulations holds out the possibility of a circumstance such as that in which Maryk acted. It is also necessary and inevitable, as spelled out in the Article itself, if there is not to be anarchy in the military structure, that the invoking of the regulation should not be taken lightly, and that the judgment of anyone acting upon it must be subjected to challenge and the burden of proof.

The court-martial does not convict Maryk, but neither does it move to lighten or mitigate the seriousness of such an action on the part of a subordinate toward his superior. To expect a military body to act other than this court acts would be romantic indeed. Maryk is justified as far as we could possibly expect within the military system.

Mr. Whyte sums it up, concerning Queeg, that Greenwald "reveals him to the court as a neurotic coward. The court acquits Maryk. Queeg's career is finished." But, he continues:

> Then the author pulls the switch. At a party afterward, lawyer Greenwald tells Maryk and the junior officers that *they*, not Queeg, were the true villains of the piece. Greenwald argues that Queeg was a regular officer, and that without regular officers there would be no going system for reserves to join later. In what must be the most irrelevant climax in

contemporary fiction, Greenwald says that he is a Jew and that his grandmother was boiled down for soap in Germany and that thanks be to the Queegs who kept the ships going. He throws a glass of champagne at Keefer.

"I see that we were in the wrong," one of the junior officers writes later, with Wouk's blessing. "The idea is, once you get an incompetent ass of a skipper—and it's a chance of war—there's nothing to do but serve him as though he were the wisest and the best, cover his mistakes, keep the ship going, and bear up."

Here, certainly, is an astounding denial of individual responsibility. The system is presented as having such a mystique that apparent evil becomes a kind of good. What would have happened if Maryk *hadn't* relieved Queeg? We are asked to accept the implied moral that it would have been better to let the ship and several hundred men perish rather than question authority—which does seem a hell of a way to keep a ship going.

Well, here equally certainly, is an astounding extrapolation from the facts of the book. How can he hold Wouk accountable for the idea that it would have been better to let the ship and several hundred men perish rather than question authority, when Wouk caused Maryk to challenge the authority, which was possibly the means of saving the ship. Moreover, it is Queeg's, not Maryk's, career which the court-martial terminates, even though the situation cannot be other than uncomfortable for Maryk and some nominal face-saving is offered to Queeg. Wouk has done no more in the trial than to indicate the fact, as cited before, that hindsight cannot prove whether or not the *Caine* would have foundered if Maryk had not acted. The key fact is, Maryk did act, Maryk was exonerated, and I challenge seriously the notion that the public that read the book and saw either the play or film did other than identify with Maryk in sympathy and respect, and conclude that, the circumstances being what they were, he had acted as he felt he must.

With regard to the defense of Queeg, after the trial, Wouk's attackers are blaming him for what should be regarded as one of the distinctions of the book, the fact that Queeg is not offered to us in simple black and white, but in the extreme complexity characteristic of all true human character (and without which he would not have been so superb an acting vehicle) and we are shown that it is quite impossible to be absolutely certain one way or the other in our evaluation of Queeg. If this were not so, Queeg would have been a mere straw man and the book would have lacked the central dramatic interest which made it possible for the play to focus on the trial alone.

It is true to a degree that Greenwald exposes Queeg to the court as a "neurotic coward." It would be more accurate to say that he reveals Queeg as a man in whom the slow-gathering forces of emotional instability had reached a crisis. We cannot assume that the Queeg of the typhoon incident is other than the climax of a long inner process in which he has not al-

ways been the same. The point is made that it is un-
likely that a man who was always an out and out
coward could have risen to command.

I do not see how Greenwald's premise can be challenged: that with all their possible faults or personal
limitations, the career men of the regular army and
navy are indeed the ones who keep the core of the
military establishment in readiness for the outbreak of
war, at which time the draftees and volunteers flood
in. And I do not see why Mr. Whyte calls Greenwald's allusion to the boiling down of his grandmother for soap one of "the most irrelevant climaxes
in contemporary fiction." It is highly relevant to
Greenwald's consciousness of himself as a Jew.
Greenwald's revulsion to the role that he must play in
the trial is due to the fact that he sees, as Wouk causes
us to see, the complexity of the Queeg situation, and
due to the fact that Greenwald also sees what Wouk's
critics either refuse to see or slur over: that a large responsibility for the shambles on the *Caine* rests directly upon the shoulders of Keefer. We will return
to Keefer in a few minutes.

Whyte lends too great a weight, in proportion to
the balance of the book, to the statement of a junior
officer about "an incompetent ass of a skipper." But
even so, there is a large area of truth in this principle,
insofar again as the specialized military system is
concerned. To obey one's immediate military superior, whether he's a jackass or not, can't be called, in
the ordinary usage of the term, a denial of individual

responsibility. The entire military system is a partial, arbitrary denial of subordinate individual responsibility. The system being "presented as having such a mystique that apparent evil becomes a kind of good," is stated by Whyte as though it applied to the normal patterns of society. But it does not. And how can it be challenged within the traditional military context?

Let's consider the case of the late General George S. Patton. We see him thinly disguised in Hersey's *A Bell for Adano*, as an insensitive, arrogant, brutal military steamroller. In his own proper person Patton became the figure of a *scandale* in the famous incident of the slapping of a hospitalized soldier. I have never been an admirer of old "Blood and Guts," and I can respond fully to the revulsion invited from us in the portrayal of him in *A Bell for Adano*. Yet neither Mr. Hersey, nor those who were so perturbed about the soldier-slapping incident, nor any of the rest of us who have something less than total admiration for the arch-military specimen, can deny the validity, indeed the necessity, of the particular talents and characteristics of Patton as he functioned as a formidable tank commander and leader of men within the special context and requirements of battle in World War II. It is this complexity in attempting to evaluate the late General Patton that must be applied to Wouk's attempt to evaluate Captain Queeg instead of accepting for him the standard simplification so characteristic of many touted war novels. Wouk shows us a complex man in a complex context. For this reason Queeg, in the full treatment that Wouk has given to him, is more real than most of the other projections of commanding officers in the generality of war novels.

It is a clear misreading and distortion for Whyte to charge that *The Caine Mutiny* "rationalized the impulse to belong and to accept what is as what should be. If we can be shown there is virtue in following a Queeg, how much more reason to welcome the less onerous sanctions of ordinary authority!"

Those two able critics, Brooks Atkinson and Walter Kerr, slurred in this citation by Mr. Whyte as "even such usually perceptive critics," did see the truth about Wouk's approach to the Queeg case.

Now to the question of Keefer. It is insisted by Whyte and the rest of the anti-Woukeans that the portrayal of Keefer is somehow anti-intellectual. But Keefer is not a symbol of anti-intellectualism. He is something very different indeed, which the critics of Wouk perhaps are not eager to recognize—he is a brilliant portrayal of the phony intellectual, whose name is legion. Keefer, the novelist, could not have written *The Caine Mutiny*. Keefer was working on a novel called *Multitudes, Multitudes*. Both as an editor and as a reviewer I have read Lieutenant Keefer's novel many times over. It is the standard pseudo-intellectual, pseudo-liberal, inversely romanticized novel about the war.

Keefer can only be used to stick Wouk with the stigma of anti-intellectualism if the critic is prepared to endorse Keefer as actually a stalwart type, or if the critic is attempting to deny that it is valid for Wouk to project a portrait of a phony intellectual, a man intellectually and morally dishonest, a man whose revolt against authority is strictly of the "let's you and him fight" variety, one who is the true organization man in the sense that he will stick his neck out only if nobody who matters is looking, a man who does not scruple to perjure and lie for his own security at the trial. Wouk is not offering us Keefer as the type of the intellectual. Greenwald has just as much claim to be considered an intellectual as Keefer has. Keefer is more, by the way, than phony intellectual, he is also the phony liberal, another familiar person of our time.

To sum up the case of Mr. Wouk, let me make it clear that this discussion has arisen as a corrective to an extreme. I do not regard *The Caine Mutiny* as the great American novel. I do not argue that it is distinguished literature. I would not even wish to deny that some of the aspects decried by its attackers do partly exist, or can be read into it. What I object to is the grossly overplayed picture of what Aldridge sneeringly calls "the good old Woukean world," the portrayal of Mr. Wouk as the repulsive and slavish spokesman for the conformist, and toadier to authority.

Much of the reaction against Wouk comes from those who have committed themselves to the novels of the lunatic-fringe view of life, both military and civilian, and who are compelled to defend their acceptance of the one view by attacking ruthlessly anyone who, like Wouk, avails himself of the almost forgotten privilege of the writer to portray the relatively normal, relatively average, in life and character. Even Count Tolstoy was not above doing it.

The world of Wouk, whatever its limitations, is at least a world of some balance and some reason and some responsibility. I will not be drawn into a discussion of the later book, *Marjorie Morningstar*, beyond saying that I regard it as an unsuccessful, unrealized, and generally mediocre book. It has in it vivid and rewarding isolated passages and characterizations, notably in the case of Uncle Samson-Aaron. But again, the detractors of Wouk are guilty of reading sinister and horrendous social implications into the book when in fact, without necessarily endorsing them, he has portrayed recognizable patterns of middle-class American Jewish life and experience. The anticlimactic career of Marjorie Morningstar has been duplicated by many a Marjorie Morgenstern, and Wouk is not necessarily making of her overly prolonged and romanticized career a *summum bonum*.

We cannot yet take leave of Mr. Whyte and of that section of his book which he calls "The Organization Man in Fiction." After the all-out assault on *The Caine Mutiny* most of the rest of his time is devoted, validly, to a criticism of the view of life represented in American popular magazine fiction and occasionally in TV drama. He also finds room to mention the "inspirational" books of the Peale genre. What I chiefly regret is Mr. Whyte's failure to take sufficient note of the marked difference in kind, basically, between magazine fiction and the so-called serious novel.

He takes some passing swipes at John P. Marquand, I think again a little unfairly. It is quite true that within almost any of his books Marquand could have sounded off in direct protest against or castigation of some aspects of the society he is portraying. But that simply is not Mr. Marquand's way. He has a right to be accepted for what he is: an extremely shrewd and perceptive recorder of the manners, mores, and values of certain well-known segments of American life, a great many of them representing the acme of conformism and the organization-man way of living. I think it is impossible to read these caustic and very funny satires and assume that Mr. Marquand is endorsing these people and their ways of life. He is an oblique satirist of what he observes. Yet it can also be said that he has a certain affection for these people, as one knowing them well, indeed rooted in them, their foibles, vices, and limitations notwithstanding. In the same way, Sinclair Lewis had an affection for many of his targets, including George F. Babbitt. Mr. Marquand simply is not a polemicist, and to paraphrase Mr. Churchill, he does not find it necessary to preside over the dissolution of the society that he observes for us.

Mr. Whyte's *The Organization Man* is a sometimes brilliant and valuable book and I am grateful for its contributions to our awareness of our own culture. It simply seems to me that as literary critic he is least effective, and that the section of his book devoted to our literature is the least adequate in scope, balance, and perspective.

Now let's turn to the utter antithesis of "the good old Woukean world," the world of the hipster as seen in Jack Kerouac's *On the Road*. The hipster is the practical nihilist. The theoretical nihilist negates life and the world in ideas; the practical nihilist, as in Kerouac's beat generation, negates life and the world in acts. As hero he is another manifestation of the Yahoo as social arbiter.

None of these real gone prophets has any trouble finding for himself an apologist and exegete among the reviewers and critics. The particular one who has lent the jet-assist to Mr. Kerouac's take-off is Gilbert Millstein, writing in the daily *New York Times* with an unusually long and markedly ecstatic review.

He says, ". . . Its publication is a historic occasion insofar as the exposure of an authentic work of art is of any great moment in an age in which the attention is fragmented and the sensibilities are blunted by the superlatives of fashion. . . ." (To which Kerouac would respond, "Wow! Man!" and "Phew!")

Millstein calls it "a major novel," bracketing it with *The Sun Also Rises*, claiming that *On the Road* will be to the "Beat Generation" what the earlier book was to the "Lost Generation." ". . . The fact is that *On the Road* is the most beautifully executed, the clearest and the most important utterance yet made by the generation Kerouac himself named years ago as 'beat,' and whose principal avatar he is."

The etymology of the hipster word "beat" is obscure. In this novel it appears to connote "demoralized," seen as an ideal. Kerouac defines it as "the root, the soul of Beatific." Millstein openly espouses the Aldridge theory about values and identifies Kerouac and his beat boys as falling within some of the categories of *After the Lost Generation.*

The narrator of *On the Road* is one Sal Paradise, who functions as a beat Boswell to a jiving Johnson. The latter is named Dean Moriarty, and as truly the central figure of the book is defined by Mr. Millstein as an "American hero-saint." Here follows a thumbnail survey of Kerouac on the subject of Dean.

Insofar as formative influences upon Dean are explained to us, it is in terms of a drunken father who had abandoned him. Then

> . . . when Dean grew up he began hanging around the Glenarm pool-halls; he set a Denver record for stealing cars and went to the reformatory. From the age of eleven to seventeen he was usually in reform school. His specialty was stealing cars, gunning for girls coming out of high school in the afternoon, driving them out to the mountains, making them, and coming back to sleep in any available hotel bathtub in town.

> . . . Dean's intelligence was . . . formal and shining and complete, without . . . tedious intellectualness. And his "criminality" was not something that sulked and sneered; it was a wild yea-saying overburst of American joy; it was Western, the west wind, an ode from the Plains, something new, long prophesied, long a-coming (he only stole cars for joy rides). . . .

Dean expounds some of his own philosophy in terms rather reminiscent of some characters in George Mandel's *Flee the Angry Strangers*. Sal puts the question to him: "You mean we'll end up old bums?"

> "Why not, man? Of course we will if we want to, and all that. There's no harm ending that way. You spend a whole life of non-interference with the wishes of others, including politicians and the rich, and nobody bothers you and you cut along and make it your own way. . . . What's your road, man?—holyboy road, madman road, rainbow road, guppy road, any road. It's an anywhere road for anybody anyhow. Where body how?" . . .

Sal says:

> There was nothing clear about the things he said, but what he meant to say was somehow made pure and clear. He used the word "pure" a great deal. I had never dreamed Dean would become a mystic. These were the first days of his mysticism, which would lead to the strange, ragged, W. C. Fields saintliness of his later days.

We draw in to the ultimate essence of Dean as we see him

> . . . standing in front of everybody, ragged and broken and idiotic, right under the light-bulbs, his bony mad face covered with sweat

and throbbing veins, saying, "Yes, yes, yes,"
as though tremendous revelations were pour-
ing into him all the time now, and I am con-
vinced they were, and the others suspected as
much and were frightened. He was BEAT—the
root, the soul of Beatific.

And now we have the definition:

That's what Dean was, the HOLY GOOF.

Sal Paradise himself is a writer (how else?) and it is
not too difficult to imagine what book Sal is writing,
especially the time when Dean "watched over my
shoulder as I wrote stories, yelling, 'Yes! That's right!
Wow! Man!' and 'Phew!' "

Sal, Dean, and their comrades are zealously performing "our one and noble function of the time,
move." They shuttle backward and forward, east and
west, north and south across the face of "the groan-
ing and awful continent," sometimes hitchhiking,
sometimes in legitimate cars, sometimes in stolen cars,
once in a fine Cadillac entrusted to them for delivery
in Chicago, which they drive crazily, sometimes at
120 miles per hour, and deliver in Chicago a total
wreck, barely able to roll.

When not riding, they are tearing around San Fran-
cisco, New York, New Orleans, Chicago, or Denver,
"dealing with the pit and prunejuice of poor beat life
itself in the god-awful streets of man." From start
to finish it's "a real going goofbang." Everybody is
mad: mad parties, mad speed, mad sex. They are

smoking "tea," occasionally sticking morphine, taking goofballs, benny, and liquor, all in a blur of maudlin philosophy. The periodic yawp is always kicks: "Ain't we gettin' our kicks, *anyway?* . . . Oh man what kicks!"

Like Dean, who is "too busy for scruples," they steal casually on a petty scale (except for cars). It's not that they're crooks, it's just that they're a little low on money, or need a car, or need kicks, so of course what do you do? And these "fine gone daddies" are "all in this together . . . everywhere I went everybody was in it together." This is hipster togetherness (the theory that the family that kicks together sticks together) with an utter vagueness as to who "everybody" is or what the "it" is that they are in.

Now Kerouac, with a peculiar and special intensity of his own, is engaged in telling the great lie about man. Sal and Dean are simply a greater extension in intensity of Mr. Bellow's Augie March. The whole thing adds up to the great American goof-off, as a source of pride.

Eternity comes cheaply here. It is found on the eyelids of a jazz musician. It was Miss Jane Russell, the well-known gospel singer, who dazzled us with the revelation that "God is a livin' doll." Now Kerouac, the hipster-theologian, in his final effusion, the closing lines of *On the Road*, tells us "that God is Pooh Bear." This is end-of-paved-road in man's long history of awe and worship.

Not only Mr. Millstein, who has elevated this artifact as if it were a sacramental object, but other critics have remarked upon the supposed beauty of an evocation of America which they have discerned in the wild careening over the face of the land. From Millstein: "There are sections of *On the Road* in which the writing is of a beauty almost breathtaking. There is a description of a cross-country automobile ride fully the equal, for example, of the train ride told by Thomas Wolfe in *Of Time and the River*." In the first place it is not the equal because it is so patently an imitation. Moreover, it is a slander of Wolfe, taken in the total context of the work of these two men. Kerouac is openly striving for some of those "Wolfean" rhapsodic effects, which even in Wolfe are not always successful. But Kerouac's America is the beautiful big land with the cretinous little people. Wolfe, on the American scene, is full of wonder, amazement, awe, and excitement. Kerouac at his best is possessed only by a hectic, maniacal, hyped-up frenzy.

Even prior to Millstein's effusions, as the publishers point out on the jacket, portions of *On the Road*, as work in progress, had appeared in *The Paris Review*, *New World Writing*, and *New Directions*, attracting much attention. Thus, as they say, *"On the Road* has achieved a certain pre-publication fame. The appearance of the complete work in book form is a publishing event of no small interest." I am informed that its sponsor was a distinguished American critic. These are the factors which make it necessary to devote as much time as I have given to this book and its view of life and man. Millstein said, "The book requires exegesis," and to some extent I have tried to provide it, but from a different premise.

On the other hand, that discerning and experienced critic, Mr. Carlos Baker, unhypnotized by Kerouac's bongo beat, observes that Sal Paradise obviously has read *The Adventures of Augie March* and *A Walk on the Wild Side*. He concludes that "Kerouac can write when he chooses. But this dizzy travelogue gives him little chance but to gobble a few verbal goofballs and thumb a ride to the next town."

On the Road is Kerouac's Hell. Dante once took us on a tour through Hell. The difference is, that Dante knew where he was—Kerouac doesn't.

In the summer, 1957, issue of the magazine *Dissent*, Norman Mailer had an article entitled, "The White Negro; Superficial reflections on the Hipster." He is too modest. These are quite profound reflections, touching on the origin and nature of the hipster as well as upon the implications of the phenomenon, which he discusses in what is, to me, a disturbingly noncommittal way.

The hipster, Mailer explains, is "a philosophical psychopath." We are offered him as "the American existentialist—the hipster, the man who knows . . . our collective condition is to live with instant death by atomic war, relatively quick death by the State as *l'univers concentrationnaire*, or with a slow death by conformity with every creative or rebellious instinct stifled."

As to his origin: "The bohemian and the juvenile delinquent came face-to-face with the Negro, and the hipster was a fact in American life." This could be worked up into a song, like "The Birth of the Blues." Mailer sees the Negro as the chief factor in shaping the behavior patterns of the Hip world. "The hipster had absorbed the existentialist synapses of the Negro, and for practical purposes could be considered a white Negro."

We have the picture of sharply defined alternatives between which contemporary youth must choose.

> One is Hip or one is Square (the alternative which each new generation coming into American life is beginning to feel), one is a rebel or one conforms, one is a frontiersman in the Wild West of American night life, or else a Square cell, trapped in the totalitarian tissues of American society, doomed willy-nilly to conform if one is to succeed.

Now what of this alleged inescapable dichotomy —hipster or organization man?—Hip or Square?—hipster or conformist? Mailer is selling it but I will not buy it. It reflects spurious alternatives under a spurious necessity.

Mailer paints for us a picture of a state of society which, he argues, compels the rise of the hipster as an inevitable product. He is supposed to live under and be conditioned by the constant shadow of three kinds of death unparalleled in past times. This is a maudlin, self-pitying premise that will not stand up to scrutiny. Death is no more imminent, or random, than ever it was. Death is an individual experience.

Each of us can die only once, and must die as a separate person. Death may strike at random in an auto accident, airplane crash, murder, war, or disease. Its possibility from atomic war is not as imminent as from the above commonplaces, though the intelligent man is aware that atomic war is one of the possibilities in the age. At any rate, in time, we each "owe God a death." It is foolish to talk of death as senseless. Death is termination: the sense or senselessness reposes wholly in the life it terminates which, as the saying now goes, may be your own. The hipster, or his apologist, can advance nothing new relative to death, its threat or proximity, as justification for the hipster pattern.

Then Mailer speaks of death metaphorically, in terms of statism, the universal concentration camp, or in terms of conformism to social patterns. Most of what I have to say about the much-cited conformism has been said in Chapter Four in the discussion of Aldridge's bewildered simultaneous quest for values and heresy.

Mailer's statement about being "doomed willy-nilly to conform if one is to succeed" is patently false, since such hipster prophets and saints as the late James Dean and the early Elvis Presley are enormous successes. Consider, too, the large sale and intemperate critical acclaim for Kerouac's novel. The fact is, hipsterism appears rather to be a short path to fabulous overnight success, fame, and fortune.

As for the matter of statism, or enforced conformity to authority, it is the free world that has the great upsurge of hipsterism, *not* the totalitarian world. Doubtless that portion of the total phenomenon which is simply adolescent (delayed or otherwise) is to be found in some measure everywhere. But Mr. Mailer has put before us an untenably sweeping and oversimplified description of the condition of man as the reality that engenders hipsterism. There are just enough elements of truth in his picture to lend it a false plausibility as a total thesis. The fact is, it is not from the *nature* of reality, but from the *loss of contact* with reality, that hipsterism arises.

Moreover, no word has known worse semantic abuse than "generation." Was there ever a "lost generation"? No. Was there a lost *set* within a generation? Yes. Is there now a "beat" generation? No. Is there a beat *set* within a generation? Yes.

This is a minority phenomenon—no less meaningful, ominous, and dangerous for all that. Yet the apologists and exegetes of hipsterism speak in terms that suggest an actual mass phenomenon.

Though I reject the sweeping assertion of necessity or inevitability of this phenomenon, I agree that there are elements in our culture that contribute to and nurture it and that these urgently need study and cure. Though I reject the assumption of near universality of these patterns among a generation, I agree with alarm that the influence or taint from the concentrated center of the hipster world reaches out through mass media and personalities to touch a dangerous number of adolescents. That is why it is at once a service in literature to define and describe hipsterism, and an act of irresponsibility to present it uncritically unless, as sometimes we are left to infer, the writer is endorsing it.

Mailer's article is valuable as description and definition, as Kerouac's book is valuable, as reflection, of the phenomenon in practice. (It should be noted that one wing of the Hip world disavows the authenticity of Kerouac as the voice of hipsterism.) Both novel and article fail, or decline, to do the job of evaluation. The novel seems totally, the article tacitly, to accept the pattern.

Mailer acknowledges that hipsterism is a doctrine of man. He appears to have an empathy with it. He concedes that its image of man is psychopathic but speculates that "the psychopath may indeed be the perverted and dangerous front-runner of a new kind of personality which could become the central expression of human nature before the twentieth century is over." In context, this is not the statement of alarm that it might seem to be. He appears to regard hipsterism as a viable life scheme, viewing it with wide-eyed interest. He seems more repelled by the Square than by the hipster.

The sense of alternative that looms so large in the discussion is because hipsterism is a polarized vision of life. You are *either/or*. It knows nothing of *both/and*. What is the meaning or definition of Square? It is all that is not Hip. In Marlowe's phrase, "All places shall be Hell that are not Heaven."

A major aspect of the hipster is that he is a sexual

rebel, and that in this area, and others, all his values are sensory values. Mailer tells us that this psychopath, this hipster, seeks love: "Not love as the search for a mate, but love as the search for an orgasm more apocalyptic than the one which preceded it." Mailer speaks extensively of successful living in terms of the attainment of "good" rather than "bad" orgasm.

Hipster love is not love at all—it is the craving for detumescence, nervous discharge, as pictured by Aldous Huxley in his undervalued novel, *Ape and Essence,* in which the love song was

> Love, Love, Love—
> Love's the very essence
> Of everything I think, of everything I do.
> Give me, Give me, Give me,
> Give me detumescence.
> That means you.

The "apocalyptic orgasm" at the center of Mailer's orgasm mystique of hipsterism is utterly isolated orgasm, unshared in the sense of being detached from personal communion with its agent-instrument. Only the potential heightening of its sensory experience by the actions of another body differentiate it from the orgasm of masturbation. Homosexual or heterosexual union will serve it equally well. As with all the other facets of the pattern, Kerouac's novel demonstrates the actuality of hipster love in all variations.

Being a creature of restless, incessant movement, in constant quest of sensation, of kicks, the hipster has a wholly relativistic value scale.

Character being thus seen as perpetually am-
bivalent and dynamic enters then into an absolute relativity where there are no truths
other than the isolated truths of what each
observer feels at each instant of his existence.
. . . What is consequent therefore is the di-
vorce of man from his values, the liberation
of the self from the Super-Ego of society. The
only Hip morality (but of course it is an ever-
present morality) is to do what one feels
whenever and wherever it is possible, and—
this is how the war of the Hip and the Square
begins—to be engaged in one primal battle:
to open the limits of the possible for oneself,
for oneself alone because that is one's need.

"Oneself alone"—the key to hipsterism, the key to
the hipster orgasm, the reason for the sometimes mo-
tiveless, senseless, remorseless hipster crime so baffling
to the onlooking Square.

Hipsterism is practicing solipsism—belief in the reality of the self alone. It is the antithesis of the life of
dialogue in which the personality is conceived as
brought into definition and identity in encounters between an *I* and a *Thou*, between man and man, or
between man and God.

Hipsterism is not, as its bards celebrate it, or as
Mailer tentatively appraises it, some kind of new
dynamic, with at least a potential of health, an alternative to conformism, a possible forerunner of a
future man. Hipsterism is disease, social and individual.
As a marginal or full-scale psychopathic condition it
needs individual therapy and, when it threatens to

be epidemic, it needs public health measures in the sense of study and treatment of those elements in our admittedly unhealthy culture which contribute most to the encouragement of such phenomena.

A contributing factor insufficiently stressed by Mailer, though not ignored, is boredom. Frenziedly intense in some small areas, in other and larger ones the hipster is the person who couldn't care less. This brings me to the phrase which, in all of Mailer's article, I find least acceptable. He speaks of "despair at the monotony and bleakness of the future." Whose future? Let him speak for himself.

The state of being bored is subjective. Life is not boring, *you* are bored. We are pictured as living under a deadening blanket of conformity, which is a gross exaggeration of the truth that, as always and everywhere, there are patterns of conformity in our culture.

The future is a composite of what we will make of it as a people and of how we will respond to it as individuals. There will be griefs and woes and possible catastrophes in the future, but there will be exhilaration and almost unimaginable adventure. *Monotony*, when man stands at the threshold of space? *Bleakness?* The challenge is directly to us, whether yes or no; there is no maudlin fatalism about it.

The great source of boredom (and for that matter of conformity) is the loss of the sense of wonder and awe, which has proceeded from the partial loss of the Judeo-Christian image of man. Wonder at his own marvellous origin and nature, and the worship of the

Creator, which this wonder impels, are what nourish the psyche of man. The deadly, spurious religion of the hipster is blighting. Mailer describes:

> . . . that God which every hipster believes is located in the senses of his body, that trapped, mutilated and nonetheless megalomaniacal God who is It, who is energy, life, sex, force . . . not the God of the churches but the unachievable whisper of mystery within the sex, the paradise of limitless energy and perception just beyond the next wave of the next orgasm.
>
> To which a cool cat might reply, "Crazy, man!"

This particular Square (I happen to be the ultimate, literally—a solid Square from Delaware) also says, "crazy," but not in the bright lexicon of Hip.

Hipster wonder is a peculiar thing, for some sense of wonder (chiefly in terms of total sensation) he does have—more than many a Square can boast. But his wonder is deformed and one-dimensional. Mailer observes that it is the peculiarity of the hipster that he lives in the present exclusively (characteristically he may insist that the dead James Dean is still alive).

There are contexts in which the ability to live in the present is important, and some personalities are malformed through a lack of this ability. But the animal lives almost exclusively in the present, too. For man, who is geared to a more complex life in time, to live too exclusively in the present soon leads to the growth-arresting, maturity-rejecting, vain effort to arrest the present—to hold the unstoppable present,

passing moment and sensation. It is the unique crea-
tureliness of man that he lives in a triple dimension of
time: past, present, future. Full self-realization as
man requires a full apprehension and proportionate
weight of each of these three aspects of our life in
time—together with an even more remarkable ability
to conceive a realm of being and Creation that stands
outside of time.

Whole man is wondering man and worshipping
man. This man has the clearest mind for examining
himself and his society and his expanding environment in the universe. He is least susceptible to, and
most curable from, those diseases of the group and
the individual to which our basic creaturely limitations, combined with the strains of a transition culture, keep us liable.

The new gullibility of our particular time is not
that of the man who believes too much, but that of
the man who believes too little—the man who has
lost his sense of the miracle—the man capable of believing that Creation is in some way an automatic or
commonplace thing, or even that man himself, physi-
cally and psychically, can be dissected into neat pack-
ages susceptible to complete explanation.

When awe and wonder depart from our awareness, depression sets in, and after its blanket has lain
smotheringly upon us for a while, despair may ensue,
or the quest for kicks begin. The loss of wonder, of
awe, of the sense of the sublime, is a condition leading
to the death of the soul. There is no more withering

state than that which takes all things for granted, whether with respect to human beings or the rest of the natural order. The blasé attitude means spiritual, emotional, intellectual, and creative death.

Abraham Heschel observes that "away from the immense, cloistered in our own concepts, we may scorn and revile everything." It is this shriveling into a concept of reality circumscribed by our neurotic selves that produces the warped vision of those novelists who scorn and revile everything.

In reinvoking, as I have done, the great Western, Judeo-Christian view of man, and juxtaposing it to other views now competing with or challenging it in contemporary fiction, I come finally to a somber fact partly responsible for the diminished image of man. Our religious life, the ultimate source, preserver, and nurturer of the great Western doctrine of man, is scorned in some quarters because of the low estate to which religious understanding and practice have sunk among many of us who profess a faith. That is not the subject of this book, but I observe ruefully that only a minority among those calling themselves, formally, Christians or Jews, have a profound and actively conscious awareness of what it is that those great religions actually teach about our nature as man. This is a major reason for the diminishing vision our recent age has had of our kind.

Whether we are Jews, or Christians, or of any other persuasion; whether we profess any religion or not, we have a need and an obligation to reappraise and refocus our vision of ourselves and our species in terms of the great tradition of man which has shaped the constructive history of our Western world, and of which we are all co-inheritors. We need to make this reappraisal in our lives and we need to make it in our literature and other arts, and in our sciences.

We need to look continually upon ourselves, our lives, and destinies, in terms of what Abraham Heschel has called "radical amazement," the alertness to awe, to grandeur, to the sense of the numinous, the holy. This radical amazement was the genius and inspiration of the Jews, found in the psalmists, in *Job*, and in the great prophets; radical amazement at creation: "The great things and unsearchable, the wondrous things without number," and amazement at man, "for I am fearfully and wonderfully made . . . and in thy book were all my members written."

Index

ABOUT THE AUTHOR

EDMUND FULLER has worked as author, editor, critic
and teacher. He has written two novels, *Brothers Divided*
and *A Star Pointed North,* as well as diversified non-fiction,
including *George Bernard Shaw: Critic of Western Morale.*
His reviews and articles appear in *The New York Times
Book Review, The Saturday Review, The American Scholar*
and the *Chicago Tribune Magazine of Books.* He has taught
comparative literature and the craft of fiction and drama at
Columbia University. Mr. Fuller is forty-four years old; his
home is in Kent, Connecticut, where he teaches at Kent
School.

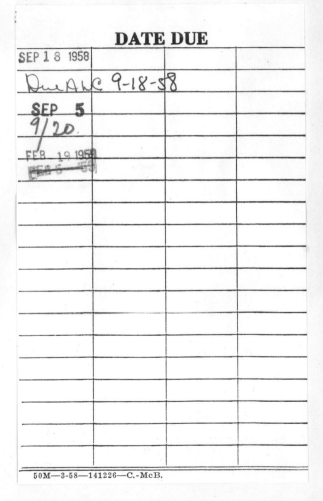

DATE DUE

SEP 1 8 1958		
Due Aug 9-18-58		
SEP 5		
9/20.		
FEB 19 1959		
FEB 6 59		